"I loved it! Thi... much soul sear... has brought cl... _y_

...aker

"Again, I am so glad Leslie shared your book with me. Although I only took it from her for a quick look, I found it hard to put down. It took us to a new level of discussion and added some nice spirituality to sitting at the pool in the city of plastic, sin, and really good croissants."

—Debbie Slevin, columnist

"I loved your ideas for living. They are clear, specific, uplifting, and liberating!"

—Sarita Crawford, English Instructor

"Truly, an inspirational story! This book is a 'lighthouse' to others. Keep up the great work you are doing! Shine the light! Shine the light!!!"

—Claudia Merwin, facilitator for fire-walk seminars

"The Spirit of Joy reminded me, once again, that the choice to alter our lives is within us. Joy, love and peace are where I want to be, and for those of us who do, this book is a must read!"

—Tara Wells, residential counselor

"This was a joy to read! It is already making a difference in how I live my life. After reading your book, I allow myself more space and am more gentle with myself. Thank you so much!"

—Jenny Briggs, massage therapist

What would you do if an attractive stranger showed up alone one night at your doorstep, offering to teach you the meaning of life?

What if the stranger claimed to be an angel—your very own?

Would you invite her in for tea, hoping for an outside shot at your own personal miracle?

It happened to me, and when I opened that door I had no idea what I was getting myself into...

The Spirit of Joy

A Transformational Journey to Awaken the Soul

CARL R. NASSAR

Published by

Miracle Books

Miracle Books ℘

a division of
The Miracle Center
141 S. College Ave. Suite 213
Fort Collins, CO 80524
www.MiracleCenter.com

For written permissions or further information address Miracle Books c/o The Miracle Center, 141 S. College Ave., Suite 213, Fort Collins, CO 80524.

ISBN: 0-9701595-2-8
Library of Congress Card Number: 00-191684

First Printing: January 2001
Printed in the USA
10 9 8 7 6 5 4 3 2

Publisher's Cataloging-In-Publication
(Provided by Quality Books, Inc.)

Nassar, Carl, 1968-
        The spirit of joy : a transformational journey to
    awaken the soul / Carl R. Nassar. -- 1st ed.
        p.cm.
        LCCN 00-191684
        ISBN 0-9701595-2-8

        1. Joy. 2. Soul. 3. Spiritualism.   I. Title.

    BJ1481.N37 2001   158.1
                                     QBI00-901373

CONTENTS

Saturday, February 9

Saturday, February 16

Saturday, February 23

ACKNOWLEDGMENTS

The Beatles once sang, "I get by with a little help from my friends." Indeed! So much in my life has been generously supported by family and friends. They have bravely encouraged me to pursue my passions. This book would not be complete if I did not take time out to thank those who so generously loved and supported me.

First, there is the inspirational woman who holds my hand as together we journey through a life of celebration and wonder. Gretchen Brooks Nassar, my life with you is, truly, a gift from God. Thank you for loving me so profoundly, and for giving me the permission to love in that way.

There is also the delightful woman who joined me in my quest to share beauty and joy through The Miracle Center. Brenda Rader Mross, thank you for your unflappable support. You are the world's greatest cheerleader. Thank you for seeing the best in me, and helping me give the world my best.

There are of course the three people who, for their entire lives, have loved me. First they gave me the greatest gift of all, my life. Then, they did the best they knew to support my love of it. Mom, Dad, and Christine, thank you for surrounding me with the best of you for so many years.

There are countless people who appeared, popping in my life at just the right moments, teaching me, and then taking leave.

They are the angels in human form who blessed my life, if only for a short time. Your collective touch lives on in me, and I am grateful for my time with all of you. You know who you are!

And then, of course, there's Joy!

Saturday

January 5

Chapter 1

First Encounters

I t all started one cold winter's day. I was walking my way to Paradigm, a quaint little bookstore hiding in the basement lot of a three-story building. Small in size, she compensated by selling only one genre of book—the how-to-put-your-life-together-when-it's-all-falling-apart genre, which publishers gently entitle "self-help."

"How did it get to this point," I asked myself, more incrimination than question, "that I'd need self-help books?" My thoughts came together, reminding me of the revelation that had come in last night's dream:

> A great king, rich in land and wisdom, was speaking to a common man. "I shall give you everything you will ever need to enjoy life. Your external world will overflow with abundance, and you will have far more than kings from times-gone-by even dreamed possible.

And so it came to pass that in the common man's life, he knew only youth and the health and vitality it brought him. He was granted both fame and fortune beyond measure. His many partners were beautiful to behold, and many a man turned his head to see the latest vision of beauty in his arms.

But despite outward appearances, and all that the king had given him, the man was dying inside. While his life knew abundance from without, it grew only in misery from within.

The man searched for a way to joy.

"I will do work that makes the world a better place," the man resolved. He imagined how his great acts would liberate him from his sadness. But the world around him was busy building weapons of war. It was not interested in his workings of peace. Easily discouraged, the man gave up this dream.

"Well then," the man decided, still seeking joy, "I will find a job and work with people who know energy and enthusiasm. Together, my coworkers and I will ride the excitement of life." But in the work that came his way, he found not what he sought. Those around him worked, oddly enough, only to escape from work.

"If all you dream of is freedom," the man asked his colleagues once, "then why not leave?"

"Well," one had replied, thinking the obvious question a rude one, "I have bills to pay, food to buy, and a family to create one day. I will barter my happiness at work, trading it in for the chance at joy elsewhere."

"But can we not have it all?" the man wondered. "Could we not love our work and all else in our lives?" Despite his questions, the day quickly came when the man surrendered to the sadness of his surroundings at work. He abandoned dreams of excitement on the job, and sought internal joy elsewhere.

"With all my fame and fortune, I can have any woman I want. I will create a relationship that will nurture my soul, and help my spirit soar," the man told himself. With the promise of hope and the vastness of possibility, he embarked on a new journey with a woman beautiful to behold. In their early days, they blossomed under the freedom of love. But fears arose, and what had been so long in creating was fast to fall. Soon, all that was left to keep them together was the fear of being alone. "Better together in misery than alone in pain," the man convinced himself, forgetting why he had believed in relationships in the first place.

Finally, the misery within grew so large that the man declared, "Something must be done!" He searched for someone to save him from his sadness. But he'd moved far from home, away from parents who had always worked hard to rid him of his unhappiness. His friends were content to help him drink his way out of misery, but that seemed too fleeting a solution. For the first time in his life, the man realized he was the only one who could save himself from the misery into which he'd fallen. "It's time," he resolved, "for self-help. It is time I journey into my soul."

That dream, and how clearly I saw myself in it, was why I now headed for the hidden land of a self-help bookstore called Paradigm. I felt a presence of abundance in my life, but still couldn't escape a misery that ravaged my soul. Work was unrewarding. My relationships were bottoming out. And it seemed there was no one to help. No one, that was, except me.

When I arrived at Paradigm, I was soothed by the flute sounds she sang to me on her speakers, calmed by the sweet aroma of the sandalwood incense that flavored her landscape. Shelves of carefully selected and neatly stacked books surrounded me: her mountains of knowledge.

"Each one here is hand-chosen by me," the creator of the Land of Paradigm shared with me proudly. "When you're small, you've got to be good, and you'll only find the very best in self-help here."

I pulled down the books whose titles lured me. On that day, *Illusions* by Richard Bach spoke to me. I glanced at her back cover and leafed through her pages.

"How is it?" I asked the owner, eager for some positive affirmation regarding my first selection. This was, after all, a self-help bookstore.

"I think you'll like it. I did when I read it," he offered weakly. Not quite the 'it'll-change-your-life' encouragement I was hoping for.

Soon, I walked out, *Illusions* in hand, and began the journey home that cold Saturday morning. It was then that it happened.

I saw *her* for the first time. And after that first moment, I couldn't stop seeing her. She moved with the gentleness of a soft morning breeze, and her every step carried with it a confidence and self-assurance unlike any I'd ever seen. Her eyes sparkled, a mesmerizing blend of serenity and empowerment. They spoke of comfort and compassion. As she moved, she lit up the world around her. At first, I thought it was her long hair reflecting the traces of sunlight that broke through the cloud-infected sky. Then, I realized her glow emanated from a source deep within: an abundance of radiance, a pool of Divinity that was as tangible as the warmth that painted her face.

Before I knew it, she was walking by. My brief moment of contact with this vision was about to become memory. "If only people had the courage to speak to each other, and not be so darn afraid of one another. Then I'd be able to say a hello," I thought to myself, my frustration growing.

"Too many TV shows about violence, too much fear in this world. So much so I can't even speak to someone on the street, not even a simple 'hi,' anymore."

I looked up at her, hoping now for a mere moment of eye contact as consolation. Suddenly, she stopped walking.

"Well, if you want to say something, just say it," she offered playfully, deciding to talk rather than walk by. Her eyes danced as she spoke, sparkling with the hidden pools of energy that live within us all.

"Oh, and a word of advice: Stop blaming the world around you for everything you fail to do. If you don't talk to me, that's your decision, not the world's fault."

I watched the sound "Wha...?" squeak out of my mouth. I was stunned. No, overwhelmed. No, in a state of disbelief. Did a beautiful, radiant woman just stop on the street and talk to me? Did she just respond to the thoughts in my mind?

She smiled, as if amused by my state of profound confusion. "Oh, and by the way," she offered playfully, pointing to *Illusions,* "great book. It'll change your life...if you let it. Just remember: We're all prophets. Being a prophet isn't an act of God, it's a choice."

With that she smiled, turned and walked away, leaving me to my confusion. I stood stunned but smiling. I don't know how long I stood there. Seconds...minutes...an hour. Time had lost its meaning. I stood in the middle of a busy sidewalk on a cold and cloud-covered day, passersby hurrying through their everyday life, occasionally jarring me with a small bump, often glaring at me for my refusal to move out of their way. But I was immune to the world outside me, and suddenly awake to a world within.

Chapter 2

Foreshadowing

When I returned home later that morning, I was cold. I must have been standing on that street corner for an hour. My ears, bright red, matched my cheeks' new color, and my hands and feet were bitingly cold.

I ran the bath water, made some tea. I entered the bathroom, Richard Bach's *Illusions* in one hand, hot tea in the other. I settled into the tub, and just before I started reading remembered her words: "Being a prophet isn't an act of God, it's a choice."

I wasn't ready for the words I read: a prophet creating vampires to make a point; a prophet bad-mouthing the public; visions of blue feathers. If this was self-help, perhaps I needed something altogether different.

But not all of the book was lost to me that day. As I continued to read, now in a robe, snuggled on my living room couch, I fell asleep. One idea, inspired by *Illusions*, came to life in my dreams.

I was living in a different land, yet one that felt frighteningly familiar. I had lived here a long time, all my life it seemed. But where was I?

I noticed a letter addressed to me in my hand: 1 Anxiety Ave., Land of Fear, USA 00000.

Of course, I recalled, the land where everyone lives much the same way, doing much the same thing, doing it in much the same manner.

Suddenly, I saw one daring soul declaring he was ready to leave the Land of Fear. He wanted to swim in the Ocean of Wonder whose calming waters lay just outside of town.

"Well, don't we all," I thought, "but we have to be realistic about it. The only way to the Ocean of Wonder from the Land of Fear is a dive off a steep cliff."

The world around him told him he was crazy. I told him he was crazy. He would be smashed and destroyed by the rocks below when he jumped off that cliff. He would never make it to the Ocean of Wonder.

"I can't keep living this way," he said. "I'd rather die trying than live another day in this joyless place."

So he walked to the edge of the cliff, the rest of the town following, pleading with him to reconsider. But his mind was made up.

He stood now on the edge of the cliff. The crowd stood in stunned silence. The minister prepared the eulogy.

When he jumped off the cliff, something very strange happened. He did not land in the Ocean of Wonder. Nor did he smash on the jagged rocks below. No, when he jumped, he found that not only did he survive, he soared. Why, he flew off the cliff and into the air, and soared on the Winds of Wonder that blew just above the Ocean of Wonder.

The people of the Land of Fear called out, "Look! A prophet, a man blessed by God. Come back and teach us, that we too might soar."

He who soared shouted back, "Oh, no, you can all do it, if only you'd find the courage to jump."

As I looked, I noticed that the man soaring was me! I had jumped!

Then, suddenly, flying beside me, was the woman from the street. "See," she said excitedly, "being a prophet is not an act of God, it's a choice."

Saturday

January 12

Chapter 3

Second Encounters

The next week I went back to Paradigm. My first experience with her brand of self-help had been a little too fantasy-like for me. I sought help more grounded in my sense of reality, and I believed that with a little more looking, I would find more realistic help in Paradigm.

Paradigm greeted me a second time with the sweet sounds of flutes and the calming scents of sandalwood. I looked once more through her small mountain of books.

"Something that would speak to me more easily. This time something less 'out there,' something rooted in the real world experience. Be more selective," I reminded myself.

Soon, I sat in Paradigm's back corner, welcomed by her rocking chair. I leafed through my pile seven books high, and, almost an hour later, emerged with my newfound treasure in hand, this time Victor Frankl's *Man's Search for Meaning.* "You can't get much more real world than a man's experience in a concentration camp," I told myself.

"How's this one?" I asked the owner as I dished out bills from my pockets in trade for the book. Again, I wanted rave reviews for my selection, a statement that my life would be changed in just a few hundred pages.

"Good choice," he offered weakly.

"I don't imagine you were ever a cheerleader in high school," I offered jokingly, hoping to bring some spark to our conversation.

"No," he said gently.

"Looks like I'm going to have to find my encouragement elsewhere," I said, meaning to say it to myself, but noticing that the words had escaped my mouth.

"You might want to consider looking inside for that," he offered softly.

"Yeah," I said quickly, now in a hurry to leave, embarrassed by my comment.

I walked out into a bitter cold winter air, leaving the sound of door chimes behind. I blinked as my eyes adjusted to the light. The sun shone proudly, manifesting blinding reflections on the frozen snow that covered the city.

"I wonder if I'll see her again," I thought, reflecting on my previous encounter with a woman of wonder. The moment I thought it, it seemed to me, it happened.

There she was again. More beautiful than the first time I'd seen her. In the brightness of full sunlight, she radiated. It was as if she reflected both the light of the outside world, and the light of some deeper, inner world. Shining inside and out, I couldn't free my eyes from her glow of pure delight.

For a moment I wondered if I was dreaming. Then, I felt the chill of the air against my face, and decided I couldn't dream of days as cold as this.

"She's not going to walk away from me so easily this time," I declared inwardly. "I've got some questions that I'd like answered."

She moved closer, in full stride, and it seemed she intended to just walk on by, a vision of wonder like none I'd ever seen. I lost myself in her radiance, forgetting what just moments ago I'd told myself with great resolve. Then, as suddenly as she had the first time, she stopped, standing right in front of me.

"Great choice," she said, pointing to my book. "Remember, all things are possible for those who believe. Believe you can choose your response, and you can."

I recovered from my initial shock enough to speak, albeit not very well. "Wait. Who are you? What are you saying? Will you come over for dinner?"

She smiled and said, "You'll see me soon enough," and without another word walked off. By the time it occurred to me that I could walk after her, she had turned a corner and was out of sight.

I continued home, wondering what was going on. "One day I decide to try self-help and now I'm seeing visions of a woman sharing riddles with me." While a part of me was frustrated, even scared, another part marveled at the great adventure I was preparing to embark on.

Chapter 4

Hope

I returned home, book in hand, images of beauty dancing through my mind, and a body chilled from the icy winter air. I'd treat myself with the warmth of a bath, I decided.

Weekdays, I hurried from bed to breakfast to shower, in a mad rush to get to a place called work, a place I couldn't wait to rush away from. The weekend was my sanctuary from that madness.

The luxury of a hot bath on Saturday was a simple beginning, telling me of my new commitment to take a little time out to care for myself. Although I didn't know it at the time, it was one of the first acts of self-help I was participating in.

I prepared a cup of hot tea, wanting to warm my body inside as well as out, and headed for the tub. *Man's Search for*

Meaning, and my hope that its few hundred pages could comfort my soul, accompanied me. Before I began to read, I remembered the words shared with me by my stranger on the street: "all things are possible to those who believe. Believe you can choose your response and you can."

"Well, if I'm going to meet a strange woman on the street who shares insights with me," I thought to myself, "I'm glad she's an optimist."

Man's Search for Meaning was a book I could lose myself in. In fact, I got so lost in its words that I forgot I was in a tub, and it took the cooling of the water and the shouts of a body shivering to jar me free from the book that held my mind hostage.

Man's Search for Meaning was just what it promised to be: one man's quest for meaning in his life. Victor Frankl, however, found a most unusual place to seek out meaning. Or, more accurately, a most unusual place to seek meaning found Victor. Victor was a Jew, a Jew with the grave misfortune of living in a Nazi Germany. He was abducted and taken to Auschwitz, the most infamous of the World War II concentration camps. There, he faced incredible misery and adversity. There, he asked himself the most profound of questions: What is the meaning of life?

It's easy to collect evidence from our surroundings to argue that life has no meaning. We can point to the nightly news and its tales of terror, or the unhappiness of our life experience, and declare that there is no reason for hope or faith or love. I should know, I've done it often enough. And Victor was given abundant opportunity to do the same—if I thought life was hell, try life in a concentration camp.

There, Victor was given every reason to lose hope. Victor could point to the fact that everything he ever worked for in his life had been taken from him. He could point his finger to a world that denied him the people he loved and cared for. He could point to the people who dictated to him what he would do from the time he awoke to the time he went to bed, the people who would shoot him if he did not do as they said, the people who treated him like a number, not human.

But Victor Frankl took the ordinary and turned it into the extraordinary. No, he did more than that—he turned the misery into meaning. He refused to believe in a life without hope, even when offered abundant reason to. Victor rose above his circumstance, he transcended the suffering around him, and he found meaning:

> *While everything may be denied me, he declared, there is one thing that nothing and no one can ever take away. I am free to choose how I will respond to the circumstances of my life. And through that freedom, my life has meaning.*
>
> *I'll find a way to respond to even the greatest of adversities with as much love as I can muster. Always, I will be free to choose to respond with love, and that freedom is my victory.*

"Victor jumped," I thought. "He took that jump from the Land of Fear and was now soaring through the Winds of Wonder. You can jump even in a concentration camp." I was inspired.

Chapter 5

Freedom

That night I had a dream. It was no ordinary dream. It was the kind of dream more real than the world that surrounds us. It was the kind of dream that comes from the soul.

"We're under attack," someone in an army uniform yelled out.

I looked around. The smell of death. The moans of pain. Visions of blood. Acts of great violence. This was war, and I was in the middle of it.

But where was I? The place seemed so familiar...my parents' house? Yes, this was their living room. There was a war raging in my parents' living room!

"What the hell are you doing?" a voice from the Persian rug yelled out to me. "Get down, grab your rifle, and fire back!"

The voice came from a very little person with a very big gun. He waved hands frantically, motioning me to drop down. Then he turned away, aimed his rifle at the enemy in the hallway, and returned fire.

I sluggishly squatted down on the patterned-rug-turned-battlefield. The little man looked at me, puzzled by my actions. "Don't you realize our lives are at stake! It's us or it's them! Now grab your gun and shoot, God-damn-it!"

It did seem like the thing to do at the time. So I picked up a gun and started firing across the few feet that separated living room from enemy hallway. "Who are we? Who are they?" I wondered. I wasn't sure it really mattered, but I wanted to know nonetheless.

I turned to the little man, his rifle still firing at unidentified hallway enemies. Their reinforcements emerged from the upstairs bathroom. He was intensely engaged in the battle. I interrupted his concentration.

"Who are we fighting?"

He looked at me for a moment, a look of utter indignation. "It doesn't matter! Fire! In the Land of Violence, it's Us or it's Them!"

He was so sure of himself, so confident that this was the right course of action, that I, unsure moments ago, let his confidence be my guide. I started firing with intention to kill. They moved closer, slinking their way through the narrow hallway, returning fire.

"They're trying to kill me," I suddenly realized, a great revelation apparent to everyone but myself.

What had I been thinking? Of course, I had to return fire. As they drew nearer, bullets tore through the bodies of my fellow soldiers on the living room carpet. A rage was growing inside. I vowed that for every one of Us they killed, I would personally kill two of Them in return.

I fired with fury. The longer this lasted, the angrier I got. A bullet caught one of the best of Us, the little man by my side. As I looked at the empty shell that had once housed his soul, a rage grew within, small at first but quickly a full-blown fanaticism.

I stormed out of the safety of the living room bunker and toward Them in their advance down the hallway. I killed ten of Them before they finally brought me down in a sea of bullets. I'd shown Them, I declared proudly, as I lay dying in my parent's living room. Everything went black in the Land of Violence.

And then…I awoke to another war zone, this time my parents' basement. I was bigger, stronger than before, better equipped for my time in this Land. A barrel of rifles lay beside me, larger, deadlier than the previous ones. I looked them over, selecting the biggest, meanest one. This time, I knew just what to do.

There, in the TV room, gunfire. I rushed over, adding my sounds of rattling bullets to the screams of warfare. I watched with pride as my bullets felled one…then two…then five of Them.

Without warning, my gun went silent. I was out of ammunition. I had to retreat, flee 'til I could grab another weapon. I ran down a short walkway that connected TV room to family room.

Someone followed. It was Them. No matter, I was a fighting machine, and I knew my way through the Land of Violence. I retreated into the long narrow passageway that led to my parents' laundry room and downstairs bathroom. Bullets screamed as they passed, none finding their mark. I dove into the basement bathroom, locking the door. There...safe at last.

My feelings of security were short-lived. It was Them at the door, quickly finding a way to pry it ajar, and in moments opening the entryway to my safe haven. They barged in, squeezing into my parents' downstairs bathroom single file, each of Them armed with heavy weaponry. I stood ground, clutching a gun without ammo, the only security I could muster in a Land of Violence.

Sometimes it is in the moments before Death that we at last find the insights we seek throughout Life. Awareness flew through my mind. Three knowings, each one ten times larger than the one before, came upon me then.

First, I understood the Law of the Land of Violence. Here, as in every land, one act of violence breeds another. Kill me now, and twenty more will rise in my name to fight Them, most crying Justice, some screaming for Vengeance. Every act of violence wouldn't end the violence, it only made it bigger.

More importantly, I understood my presence in the Land of Violence. I could only be here by my own choosing, and could only leave of my own accord. No one kept me here—I had free will. Soon after I arrived in this Land, I found myself addicted, swept up, by the world around me. Turning the rage of the Land into a rage in my heart. I embraced the violence. I wanted to use it even after it killed me, because I wanted violence to keep killing Them. So I kept coming back to this God-forsaken Land, even in death.

I thought of the irony and futility of this Land, and my role in it. So this was Violence.

The third insight arrived as a question. Do I really want to live lifetime after lifetime in violence? Is my vision of justice so warped, my call for vengeance so blinding, that I will never allow myself to see the Sea of Peace, nor the Islands of Love, nor the Mountain Tops of Hope?

No! I don't want that! There is only one way for me to end this cycle of hatred, and leave this God-forsaken Land. I must decide to never again be a part of it. I must forgive, accept, and know compassion. I must look beyond Us and Them, and see only Us.

In that very moment of wondrous vision, enemy bullets riddled my chest, flying through my body as they tore insides out. Everything went black.

My eyes opened to a bright white light shining around me. I squinted, a weak attempt to adjust. A voice spoke not in words but through my mind. "Welcome home." They were some of the warmest, most welcoming words I had ever heard.

Beside me I felt the presence of another. I turned. It was a woman. That woman! The very same radiant, glorious woman, smiling at me! "You see," she said, "believe you can choose your response and you can. Believe you can, in a moment, give up your addiction to self-inflicted violence, and you can. Believe in your peace, and it is yours."

I awoke, the awareness of my dream still my reality. I grabbed for pen and paper, but there was none by my bed. I stumbled clumsily out of the room, heading for the study. My shoulder unexpectedly encountered a wall. "Ow!" I shouted, continuing my way to my desk. Arriving at last, I began to write feverishly.

> Is my misery in life my own doing? Do I nurture unhappiness in my life the way I nurtured violence in the dream?
>
> Perhaps no one could make me miserable without my consent. Just like in the dream—no one made me violent, I had done it of my own accord.
>
> If what I'm writing is true, then I can put an end to my misery. But how?
>
> Well, how did I put an end to the violence in my dreams? I simply decided not to participate in it anymore...

I was onto something, something big. I could feel it, my whole body, my mind, even my soul, was excited.

> But how do I decide to stop participating in the misery?

Somewhere, from a place deep inside, I heard a whisper. "First," it said, "you have to understand why you became involved in the misery in the beginning."

Chapter 6

Welcome

I sat in silence for a moment, letting the calm of what must have been the middle of the night soothe my racing mind. The questions and my answers, inspired by my dream, sat quietly on paper before me.

Then I heard it. At first I thought it must be imagined, so I ignored it all together.

Then, it came again. I didn't want to believe what I was hearing, so I pretended it wasn't happening.

When I heard it for the third time, there was no denying the reality of the experience. Someone was knocking at the door...in the middle of the night!

Who would be knocking at the door at this hour? I was scared, and reasonably so, I argued. I didn't live in the best parts of town. My fear led me from the likely to the unlikely to the unbelievable: some drunk stumbling over from the bar across the street...some local kids looking for excitement...local kids high on drugs, looking for money for their next fix...with a gun...robbing me...beating me...killing me. There was no way I was answering that door.

The knock came again. And again. And again. Whoever it was, they weren't going away. Despite my best efforts to ignore them, they were not easily discouraged. My mind played in a world of possibility...a coworker who had car trouble coming home from a night out...an emergency at work and someone was dropping by to pick me up...a neighbor with a medical crisis...

The reality of it could be no worse than my fear of the unknown. "Just open the door and get it over with," I finally resolved.

I headed down the narrow, steep stairwell that lead to my front door. Whomever it was must have heard me coming, because the knocking finally gave way.

I stood on the inside of the door and shouted loudly, "Who is it?" No reply. I repeated my question, this time more demanding than the time before. Again, no reply. Resolving to get it over with, ready for the worst, I opened the door.

"Hello. I understand you have some questions you wanted answered?" There she was, my beautiful woman from the street, calm and confident. She was radiating a glow of other-worldly wonder.

Dismay gave way to delight. There was a beautiful woman at my door! My heart jumped.

But my body still raced, and my mind wanted her to know that terrorizing me in the middle of the night was not going to be an effective meeting strategy in the future.

"Did you have to scare me like that? Knocking on the door at this time of night?" I shouted, my adrenaline rush revealed in my tone.

"Well," she offered, speaking softly and sincerely, "I had considered materializing in the middle of your study and saying 'hello,' but I thought that would scare you all the more. And your desire for answers was so strong, I didn't think it wise to wait until that intensity subsided.

"Besides," she concluded, "it isn't the middle of the night, it's a new day. In your time, it's 6:30 a.m."

In "my" time? She had just considered materializing in the middle of my study? There was something very strange about this woman, and while my mind wanted to slam the door and lock her out, my heart and soul wanted more of her radiance. There was something soothing about her presence. I went with my heart and soul, ignoring the pleas of my mind. It was a decision I would learn to make again and again.

"Well, since your only alternative was beaming into my study," I offered playfully, deciding to go along with her absurdity, "then I'm glad to see you at the door. That alone scared the hell out of me."

"I know," she said, "you can be a fearful man."

I suddenly felt embarrassed by my fear. Here I was dreaming of leaps off cliffs into oceans of wonder, dreaming of letting go of violence in the middle of war and declaring peace in the face of death, and I had been terrorized by the knock on the door.

"Don't judge yourself over it," she said, as if reading my mind, "it's just what you know to do now. One day soon, you will learn a new way, an experience beyond fear."

I wasn't ready for her words, so my mind took the conversation back to something simpler.

"Who are you? How do you know where I live?" Despite my embarrassment over my fear, I was scaring myself all over again. Fear whispered in my ear, "Maybe she's some crazed stalker; maybe she's carrying a gun." But then, all she was wearing was a green jumpsuit, and there was no place to hide a gun in *that*.

"Invite me in, and I will gladly tell you all you wish to know," she announced in response to my questions.

I hesitated, then decided not to think about it and just did what felt right.

"Please come in," I said warmly. "Would you like some tea? It's cold out."

Chapter 7

Beginnings

She glided up the stairs, more floating than walking, I thought to myself. It was as if motion was suddenly artwork, and she the grand master, painting inspiring strokes with her every move.

At its top, the stairwell opened itself into the living room, where she made herself at home, sitting relaxed on the long couch.

I excused myself for a moment, mumbled "I'll be right back," and hurried to the kitchen to put a pot of hot water on the stove. In the back of my mind, I feared she might be gone as suddenly as she had appeared. So I returned as quickly as I could, delighted to find her just as I had left her, a radiant glow in my living room.

"Come in," she offered gently, as if she were not only inviting me to my living room, but into a whole new world of possibilities. "You had some questions you wanted answered."

There were so many questions that they mugged me all at once. I had no idea where to begin, so I started with what was simplest.

"Well, I have no idea what to call you..." I paused, waiting for her to take over our conversation with a simple declaration of her name. But, as I was quick to find out, nothing with this woman was handled in the usual way.

"What would you like to call me?" she offered as a soft reply.

"What would I like to call you?" I echoed, the seeds of frustration evident in my words. "Well, I'd like to call you by your name." At 6:30 a.m., I wanted her to make things easy for me.

"Yes," she said calmly. "But many people call me by many very different names. I wouldn't know which to share with you. I think it best if you decided what it is you would like to call me."

She paused a moment, leaving me for her thoughts, and upon returning offered, "Take a moment, attend to the tea, and when you walk back to the room, upon first seeing me, call me the first name that comes to mind."

Had it been anyone else, I would have at the very least turned in frustration and shared evidence explaining why it was time for her to leave: "It's 6:30 in the morning," "I don't like strangers just coming over," and, "You're being difficult."

But she spoke with such calm and sincerity that, despite the absurdity of her words, I never doubted their truth. Oh, I wasn't ready to believe them myself, but I was sure *she* believed every word she spoke. Her gentleness and simple honesty disarmed my frustration.

Responding to the pot's whistle, I left her and returned to the kitchen. My mind played with names for my newfound stranger. Ayla, from *Clan of the Cave Bear*, came to mind, where it stayed. Yes, I declared inwardly, Ayla it will be. I poured the hot water into two cups, added a small bag of tea to steep in each, and returned, cups in hand.

I arrived in the living room, handed her the tea, and was ready to name her "Ayla," when I was again overwhelmed by her presence. She smiled at me, and as quickly as they came, I forgot the earlier ramblings of my mind, losing them in the warmth of her glow. To see her was somehow to see the embodiment of Joy; living breathing Joy.

"What name came to you?" she asked, as I moved into the comfort of a plush living room chair.

"Joy," I said, speaking without thinking, sharing thoughts straight from my heart.

She rewarded me with another glowing smile. "Excellent," she replied. "Now, is there anything else I can answer for you before we begin?"

"Begin? Begin what?" I asked in tones of surprise.

"All things in the fullness of their time," she answered elusively. "But first, other questions you might have about me?"

I didn't know what to ask, and I wasn't sure I wanted her answers even if I did. Just her name had been its own adventure. But, then, questions came to me in mobs.

"Who are you? Do you know me from somewhere? Why are you here?" hurried off my lips.

"One at a time," she offered gently. "Which one first?"

"Who are you?"

"That is perhaps the most profound question of all," she began, words as soft as snow. "We are all Expressions of the Divine, Images of that which is Everything. We are reflections on the water of the great Sky." It was as if she spoke this way every day, but, seeing the puzzled, almost disappointed look on my face reminded her that I did not, and she quickly changed course.

"But perhaps that is not the answer you wanted, nor the one you are ready to hear right now," she offered. "Sometimes I get a bit ahead of myself.

"Excuse me," she offered next, "I am just so ready for you to see what has been staring you in the face for so long, I forget that opening eyes to Light, no matter how wondrous, can take time."

A part of me was unsure what she was saying, while another wondered why her every word seemed so familiar, calming my soul.

"I am, in the best words I can think ... an earth spirit ... your earth spirit. I have been with you from the beginning, a gentle guide through your life."

She spoke with such self-assurance, and such clarity, that despite my mind's best efforts, I found myself unable to doubt her words. Besides, I told myself, comforting my mind, what harm can it do to play along with her illusions? My mind relaxed, and asked what came next.

"What exactly is an earth spirit?"

"Well, this might sound a little different, perhaps a little new to you," she said, as if somehow everything else before this had been perfectly routine.

"Whenever someone is born into this expression of space-time..." she paused for a moment, as if preparing to speak in a new way. "Whenever someone is born..." she began again, pausing this time as a small self-congratulation for getting the words out the way she wanted, "the Universe offers them an abundance of loving support. She sends to you, to be with you for all this lifetime, earth spirits...earth angels...to guide you to the wonders of life."

"And you're mine?" I inquired skeptically.

"One of them," she replied, matter-of-factly, as if this was common knowledge.

"There are more of you?" I said smiling, suddenly entertained by the possibility of it all.

"Oh, abundance," she said. "Abundance, after all, is the law of the universe...for those who believe."

"Well, if that's true, why haven't I seen you before?"

"You've never looked," she replied simply enough. "Why, it's been so long you've even convinced yourself that you've forgotten how to look at all."

This was all a bit much. Let's find out what she wants and get her out of here, my mind argued. Neither heart nor spirit were opposed to finding out what she wanted, but both wanted to wait for her answer before deciding what to do next.

"So, why, then, are you here? Why can I see you now, sitting on my living room couch?" I inquired.

"You called me," she said confidently.

I found myself wishing for her longer replies again.

"What do you mean, 'I called you'?"

"Well, one day, while I was working on nurturing the rose that is the expression of your soul on a different plane of existence, I heard you call for me. You were saying...you had suffered long enough...you were tired of all the misery in your life...for the first time you were going to find your own way out.

"Don't you remember? You shouted 'Whatever it takes, whatever it is I have to do, even if it kills me, I'm going to find a way out of this misery.'

"In that moment, your mind aligned with your heart and soul, and you declared to all the Universe that you were ready to manifest...to give birth to...a new you. You were going to cease to exist in the old way, and were going to, through the sheer act of will, create a new way.

"I heard you," she continued, her voice suddenly dropping to almost a whisper, "and...I came to help."

Something she said—or was it the way she said it—touched such a deep place inside, igniting memory. Yes, I had said it, just the way she described. I remembered that day all too well. I had sat in the depth of despair that Saturday morning, tears threatening to blur my vision. From my mind's eye, I looked out into my life at that moment and saw nothing but a barren landscape. I felt desperate, ready to give up.

Some people say that the times of greatest adversity are our greatest opportunities for growth. I don't know. All I knew then was that I wanted to be anywhere and everywhere but in the barren landscape of my life.

In that moment, I knew I had a choice – I could wallow in the depths of misery, or I could begin to climb my way out. It was that morning that I said those words, "Whatever it takes, whatever it is I have to do, even if it kills me, I'm going to find a way out of this misery." I said it again, and again, and again, louder each time, until I was shouting the words out.

I went to Paradigm that day, for the very first time. I met Joy that day, for the very first time.

I had not let myself cry that day. I was too scared that once I started, I would never stop.

Now, Joy in front of me, I let the tears come. They started slowly, trickling lightly at first, but quickly moved into deep sobs...I thought of my relationship gone awry...of the time when my partner and I once knew such joy and love...and of the way it was now...me, alone on a cold beach, looking out at a barren ocean, always inviting my partner to stand by my side, always listening to her reply..."No."

I thought of work...all the long hours spent at my desk in college, full of hope and faith in my future to come, a spirit excited by the world of possibilities...and of my work now...coworkers sharing unhappiness in their daily experience...getting it all done regardless of expense to personal well-being...they even asked me to build weapons of war, when I had promised myself I'd be a man of peace...and I agreed...where was the joy in life, where had it all gone? Where was her meaning? The tears came now in buckets, and I sobbed uncontrollably.

"Good," said Joy softly, her eyes glowing orbs of compassion, "we cannot move forward, until you see, and *feel*, where it is you are now."

It must have been a good half-hour before I emptied what had felt like my lifetime supply of tears and sadness. When the sobs subsided, I felt a surprising clarity.

I looked out the window. A new day dawned, the sun inching over the horizon, painting the sky visions of wonder. A city lit up, a shining jewel dwarfed by an amber, glowing orb.

I turned to Joy, still sitting on the couch, a look of warm embrace coloring her face. She emanated calmness and clarity, seemingly undisturbed by my tears, as if somehow they were an everyday occurrence. She spoke without words, through expressions of glowing eyes, "I'm here. It's all right. It always has been. It always will be."

I closed my eyes and allowed myself a rare experience—the discovery of myself in a moment. I was breathing deeply, far more so than usual, in calming gentle rhythms.

As I probed deeper, it felt as if floodgates within, once holding strong to keep my growing unhappiness locked inside, had finally broken open. Feeling had burst through, flooding my face, and now receded into a pool of calm.

Most of all, there was a feeling of freedom. There was suddenly room inside, room made possible when I released the oceans of sadness. It was a room I could now fill with whatever I wanted. I felt ready to fill my insides with nothing but the radiance that colored the room around me.

A thought in my mind leapt forward, suddenly capturing my attention, distracting me from my newfound clarity. "You've been holding back these tears for how long?" A neighboring thought jumped in. "Why did you keep all this pent up misery trapped within?" The thoughts' questions felt more like indictments.

"You were afraid that once you began to feel your sadness, it would never stop," a new thought spoke, answering earlier questions. "And now, after thirty minutes, you feel cleansed! You waited all this time, trapping your unhappiness inside, where it grew and festered, when all along you could have cleansed yourself...in thirty minutes!" The latest thought came in the harsh tone of incrimination.

But I felt too good to trap myself in the misery of my own mind. Instead, I laughed at the irony of it all. Indeed, I had waited...I didn't know how long...weeks?...months?...years? ...keeping my sadness bottled up inside, fearing that if I set it free it would last a lifetime. Instead it came and left in thirty minutes!

I looked over at Joy, feeling I understood the meaning of her presence here this morning, feeling that she had already given me the greatest gift of all: her loving, accepting energy.

In that moment, I felt done with misery forever, ready to thank Joy for her appearance in my life, and ready to set her free.

"Set me free?" she spoke, reading my mind, amusement covering her face. "But my sweet friend, we have only just begun."

"I'm feeling so good, so alive, so free, you can't imagine!" I said, forgetting who it was I was talking to. "It's as if a giant anchor, tied to my ankle, was dragging me down. And at long last it's been cut loose. In this moment, there's nothing I can't do!"

"Wondrous," she responded. Then, inviting me to probe more deeply, she asked, in tones of curiosity and exploration, "Can you feel this way when you go into work, and see the discontent of coworkers? Can you feel this way while doing the work you call drudgery?"

I left her, lost in thought for a moment.

I imagined walking into work, a picture of myself opening the office door with zeal, walking in with my newfound energy and enthusiasm for life. Then I imaged my colleagues, looking at me strangely, wondering what was wrong with me that I was feeling good on the job. Next, I felt the misery of my coworkers surrounding me, and the slow movement of time as I engaged in activities that were of little interest to me.

"I could probably last about ten minutes at work," I announced at last, disappointed that my newfound clarity could be so fleeting.

"Every journey," she offered in response, "begins with a single step, and you have just taken your very first. If your very first step gives you ten minutes of joy a day, then in only 150 more steps you'll find happiness all day long," she offered.

"Do you mean I have to cry another 150 times?" I announced loudly, exasperated by the size of the number.

She laughed at the absurdity of the idea. "Oh no," she said. "We have a most wondrous journey ahead of us. But before we begin, we were best off starting with your announcement of where you are here and now. And you did a most wonderful job of it." She shared another smile. "After all, how can a person find his way through a city, never mind navigate his soul, when he doesn't even know where he is to begin with?

"You have begun with a very significant first step. Feeling and experiencing where you are. From here, we start a journey joy-ward."

Chapter 8

Greatest Teachers

I'll return every Saturday," Joy announced after a long pause, "for travels to your greatest teachers."

"My greatest teachers?" My mind filled with images of white light, and soft yet commanding voices. As I heard the words, whatever they would be, I imagined them echoing through me for all time, and I forever happy.

"Silly, silly, sweet man," Joy said, replying more to thought than words. "What you don't understand is that what you have just imagined lives inside you—it always has. Within you resides your image of white light, speaking words of Wisdom from all the ages. It is just that you have forgotten to listen.

"The teaching for you is not the Wisdom. It is remembering that the Wisdom is and has always lived inside you. It *is* you.

"On our journeys, you will be given opportunity to create a new vision of yourself, a vision that empowers you to hear what spirit is shouting to you from within and with-out, on every mountain top."

I wasn't sure I understood everything Joy said, nor that I believed what I did, but the softness of her words, and the assurance that I would see her every Saturday were enough for me now. My body and soul sat relaxed. My mind still wanted to know where it was we were going.

"Where are we going each Saturday? You said it was to my greatest teachers, and by that you meant ..." I paused, waiting for her reply to fill the silence.

"Experience," she said. "Your greatest teachers are experiences."

"You see," she began, launching into a story ...

> Once upon a time, and what a time it was, there lived a king, no ordinary king. He was king of a great land, a land which spanned as far as the eye could see. The kingdom he ruled was known as The Kingdom of Soul.
>
> The King had Everything, and knew only the experience of Unity and Abundance and Wonder.
>
> One day, the King decided he would play in his Land, his Land of Infinite Possibility, a part of the Kingdom of Soul.
>
> "But where in the land shall I go to play?" the King asked himself.

"Well, what do I wish to experience?" the King responded, answering his own question with yet another.

"I want to experience Love," the King decided at last, "the truest part of all that I am."

"Ah," he declared, "then I shall create a land where from the moment I appear I shall be loved forever by all that is. There will be no one who will not adore me, and everyone will know only the greatest love for me."

"But I already know that experience of Infinite Love here," the king told himself, "in the Kingdom of Soul. So why create the exact same somewhere else?"

"That just won't do," he concluded.

Then the king had the most delicious idea, and his face lit up with his thoughts of fascination and wonder. "What if, and I know this sounds crazy," the king whispered to himself, "what if I create a place where when I enter ..." He pulled out a pen, and began to write this list:

1. I will create something new, space and time.

2. When I enter space-time, I will forget...forget that I am Love, a part of Divine. (If I enter remembering, then all I will know to do is live Love, and I will be where I am now. Yet I crave a new experience to delight in.)

3. In each moment of time, I will create opportunities to discover Love, as if it were something new to be found.

4. To discover Love, I must first hide it somewhere. (But where? If I hide it on the mountain top, then

surely I will build climbing tools and find it with ease; if I hide it on the ocean's bottom, then surely I will build big machines to find it there too…but then where…)

The king's eyes lit up with inspiration as he continued to write…

5. I will hide the wonder of who I am…within… inside of me. And I will create a world where everyone tells me to look outside of myself for that wonder.

6. In each moment of time, I will give myself…experience. Each experience will be something that appears from the space outside of me. It will seem to me as if it were not of my doing.

7. Each experience will be my personal opportunity. In it, I will be able to decide; always I will have one choice. I can remember the fullness of Who I Am, the Love that I am, that lives within me. Or…there will have to be an opposite experience, a new possibility. To forget who I am, I will create experience the opposite of love. I will call it…Fear.

8. Each experience, then, will be my opportunity, to choose between Love and Fear. To remember the truth of who I am or to forget.

Delighted, the king of the Kingdom of Soul hurried to this new land of his own creation…

"You, and each and every one of you sweet people who color this planet," Joy continued, enunciating carefully, wanting to make sure I heard and understood every word, "you are that

King. You have *created* experience. Experience *is* your greatest teacher. Experience *is* your opportunity. You create experience after experience for yourselves, a new one in each moment, always to *create* through it the Awareness of who you are; always to *create* through it the Love that lives within you.

"And if you do not choose the Love in one experience..." she went on, pausing often to give me time to understand, "...do not worry. You have a new moment of experience facing you, a new gift, always, a new hope."

"And, of course, you are always free to go back to an old experience and know the love that you missed then...now."

"I will come to you every Saturday, and we will go back to old experience...so that you can look, see and learn, if you choose." The way she spoke, the story she spun, it all sounded so wondrous, as if somehow she was going to take me...*home*. Home to the feelings of love inside that I always said I wanted in my life.

"I can't wait!" I exclaimed.

"Good," she replied.

Suddenly, her tone turned very serious. "But you must know this. I can do nothing for you but present you with opportunity. Only you can take it, and transform it into magic in your life. All true teachers know this...there is nothing you can teach a student who is not ready to learn, and nothing you cannot when the student is ready."

"Even with words like a cheesy fortune cookie," I thought, "when she speaks them, she spins them into gold."

"I'm ready!" I declared, her words building my resolve.

"One last thing. In all things of great value there is great risk. In journeying with me, everything in your life will be the same, and yet to you it will be completely different. You must be willing to give up the world you know now...everything."

Her words, and the eerie warning they conveyed, sent a shudder through my body. My mind was having second thoughts. My soul spoke before my mind could object.

"Yes," I said, "I've been ready for a very long time."

"Good," she said.

She stood up, supremely confident in her every move, and headed for the door. I wanted to ask her where she was going, what time she would be back, was there somewhere I could reach her. But, for some reason, I didn't. I knew we were done for this night, and that she would be back next Saturday, when she was ready.

I watched her glide through the living room, heard the gentle patter of footsteps down the stairs, and then a soft opening and closing of the door.

"What have I just gotten myself into?" I wondered, fear returning in her absence.

Chapter 9

Quiet Moments with a Stranger

Next Saturday couldn't come quickly enough. The week between was fast becoming an exercise in futility.

"If I'd really listened and embraced Joy's words," I told myself, indicting myself with my tone, "then I would find more in my everyday experiences."

I knew now, somewhere, somehow, hidden from my vision, lay a world beneath the one I saw, a world of opportunity. Every moment, each experience, was a chance at love. But while my mind entertained the possibility, and my soul delighted in it, I still had no idea how to see it.

Rush hours through traffic were still experiences in frustration. "Drivers are still mostly plain out idiots," I reiterated, telling myself what I'd heard a thousand times before.

"My boss is still intolerable, and my coworkers, through their example, still show me how to go through the motions of life, and not live one fully," I declared inwardly at work.

"I'm still that unhappy, angry man," I told myself, "one who still can't see his way out of his own misery." Convincing myself of my painful reality, I pushed through the week, awaiting the promise of Saturday.

That Friday afternoon it occurred to me that I had no clue when on Saturday Joy would come. An idea struck me then, and I knew I had to act. I pleaded my way out of work, leaving an hour early, and with excitement for the weekend to come, hurried straight to my new old-friend, Paradigm.

Paradigm was consistent, and I liked that about her. Her speakers always greeted me with music that calmed a mind ravaged by a day at the office; her sandalwood incense always soothed an often-neglected soul; and her books held the promise of tomorrows unexplored.

I shifted through the mountains of Paradigm, seeking books from seekers who had found, finding books telling of journeys into knowing. I had no idea what exactly I was looking for, but a part of me trusted that when I saw it, I would know.

Then, on the bottom shelf, a book called my name.

"Pssst. Over here," he shouted. I looked around, but saw nothing. "Down here," he screamed, unable to wait to be noticed. I looked down, and there, hidden in the bottom shelf of the bookstore was a book, speaking to me in imagined words.

"Pick me up, take a look," he said proudly, shining his new black cover in my direction. He looked good, sharply dressed in fact. My eyes went straight for his title. *Way of the Peaceful Warrior.* I liked the sound of him: a warrior on this journey, some great noble gladiator out to conquer the demons of his soul, so at last he could know the joy that had eluded him through the years.

Next, I read his subtitle. *A Book That Changes Lives.* I was angered by its audacity. I prepared to put the book back where it belonged, out of my hands and in a well-hidden bottom shelf.

"Wait!" the book cried out. "Just open my pages!"

It was a desperate attempt. Deciding it could do no harm, I opened him up, ready to give him only the slimmest of chances.

Inside his front cover lay pages of testimonial. Not from the *New York Times Book Review*, nor the *San Francisco Chronicle*, nor *USA Today*. No, these were reviews from everyday people—Jan, the homemaker, Bill, the construction worker, Don, the Engineer. Each thanked Dan, telling how his book touched a life, transformed experience, uprooted history.

The book had my undivided attention.

"See," the booked piped. "Take me home with you."

Intrigued, I took him with me for further inspection, walking to the rocking chair in the back of this small room turned

Land of Paradigm. I read his words and liked him immediately. Simple writing. Story-telling. Dialogue. And most of all, a tale of Dan Millman's awakening to the world of possibility, inspired by old-man teacher Socrates. I wanted to know his journey, hoping it would foreshadow mine. The booked smiled at me, relieved.

"And this one?" I inquired at the front desk, pulling out my credit card when I realized I had no money in my pockets. I was hopeful that the owner would at last give me his blessing, his assurance that this book would turn a life, my life, around.

He smiled in reply, as if deciding I didn't need *his* answer to know the value of *my* book. We sat in silence, the credit card machine deciding she had all the time in the world to process. I experienced the awkwardness of a quiet moment with a stranger, while he looked surprisingly comfortable, as if enjoying quiet time with an old friend.

When at last a piece of paper popped from the credit card machine, I quickly signed it, then headed out. I jumped in my ocean-blue Toyota and raced home, hoping to beat the traffic, new treasure in hand.

Saturday

January 19

Chapter 10

Prelude to Joy

The morning light, squeezing through a small crack in my bedroom blinds, tapped my shoulder, awakening me from my slumber. My mind jumped with realization while my body arose sluggishly.

It was Saturday, glorious Saturday! Joy was coming today! She would take me away from it all! She would take me on a journey of discovery, through space and time. My mind was so excited that it coaxed my body into leaping out of bed, despite the 6:45 glow on my alarm clock display.

I hurried to the living room, hoping to find Joy relaxed on my couch, sitting just as I had seen her a few days earlier. But there was no Joy there. I searched the house, ready to be startled any moment by her presence. But she was nowhere to be found. The study, the kitchen, and the bathroom each offered no Joy.

"No matter," I thought to myself, undeterred by her absence. She would be here soon enough. It seemed I had been waiting all my life for someone like this. I could wait a few more hours.

I readied a bath, quickly becoming a Saturday ritual, and soon entered, breakfast in one hand, book in the other. I satisfied the cravings of a body with cereal, toast and tea, and the callings of a mind and soul with *Way of the Peaceful Warrior.*

Every few minutes I interrupted the words on a page and the steady flow of food from hand to mouth with a quick check. I listened for any signs of the coming of Joy. But every time I checked, there was neither sound nor sight suggesting her presence.

Soon, *Way of the Peaceful Warrior* captured me, I becoming a prisoner to her spirited storytelling. I read even as the bathwater told me she was running out of heat. I read even as my body pleaded with me to move to a warmer place. I read until I could bear the cold no more.

Finally, breaking free from the captive spell, I pulled myself out of the tub, dried myself and dressed. It wasn't long before I once again allowed myself to be taken hostage, this time in the living room. There, I lay on the couch, devouring one page, then the next, as if somehow I was a starving man and the book a feast to my soul.

Soon, it was done. *Way of the Peaceful Warrior* would be the best self-help I would find for a long time in the mountains of Paradigm. Its tale of one man, Dan, and his journey of transformation, left me breathless.

Two trips on Dan's journey struck me that day: one scared, the other inspired.

First was "Dan on a boulder." This story begins and ends with Dan seated on a large rock, and in between beginning and end is time spent waiting for insight to come.

Dan leaves his rock on occasion, each time a new realization in hand, but Socrates dismisses one, then the next, and the one after that: "Insufficient." At last Dan returns with a statement of wisdom as simple as it is piercing: *There are no ordinary moments.*

"I don't want to sit on a rock for days," my mind declared, fearful that Joy would ask the same of me. "That's no way to find enlightenment!" a thought piped out. "That's no way to journey to joy!" a neighboring thought concurred. "There's no adventure in sitting," a final thought announced. Suddenly, my mind wasn't so sure she wanted Saturdays with Joy.

My mind began to race, jumping between her thoughts like a monkey swinging wildly from one vine to the next. "*Karate Kid!*" one thought exclaimed. "Remember those countless days with little friends, acting out favorite scenes from the blockbuster movie," a nearby thought reminisced, "staging imaginary karate showdowns, always ending in a climactic one-footed kick, the movie's pinnacle of daring and persistence."

Suddenly, a very different scene in the movie jumped to mind. "Remember the ancient Chinese Master, and his student painting the fence, sanding his house, for days (or was it weeks?)," a thought offered. "That student was experiencing the mundane, the most routine of the ordinary," another thought continued. "Yes, it appeared an exercise in futility, but appearances were deceiving," a wise thought reminisced. "One day the master showed the student that in the very ordinary lived the most extraordinary. The painting of the fence and sanding of the house taught the young student the very karate moves he desperately sought to learn."

"Is that my destiny with Joy?" a fear-based thought inquired. "Is she going to take me to the mundane, so I see that liberation is at hand when I change my perception of the routine?

"I hope not," a final thought announced. "The last thing my life needs is more ordinary experience. Work, and the routine of my life, are providing me with plenty as it is."

Then, I remembered the part of *Way of the Peaceful Warrior* that filled me with more hope than any fear I could create. One day, walking down the street, passing people as if obstacles to be avoided, Dan looked and saw far more than what was routinely there to see. He saw people not as "who they thought they were," but for "who they really were." He saw Divinity in motion, having a human experience. He saw Divinity forgetting the truth of who She really was. He saw Divinity playing make-believe, pretending to be shopkeeper and business woman and cab driver. With this vision, Dan saw the truth beyond the usual illusions of the world: It is not what you do that matters, it is how you do what you do that matters most. It is doing in a way that recreates the awareness of Divinity. It is not the size of the act, but the size of loving in it.

"Now that," I told myself, "is what I want Joy to show me."

It was late afternoon now, and the sun was preparing to adventure to the other side of the planet. "Too soon," I thought to myself, "but that's the reality of a winter in the Northeast." I readied myself for the coming darkness, and hoped that Joy would be here soon. I was tiring of the wait.

Dinnertime came with no signs of Joy, so I ate in solitude, the sounds of talk radio my substitute for company. After dinner I waited impatiently for her arrival, checking the window every now and again, hoping to catch sight of her as she walked down the street and toward my front door. No Joy.

It was getting late, and by 8:00 p.m. I started wondering whether she would show up at all. My mind played tricks with my impatience. I started to wonder if the whole thing had ever really happened in the first place. In that moment, Joy seemed like a dream, and I some fool for believing in her reality.

By 9:00 p.m. I'd convinced myself that Joy had never happened, explaining her away as figments of imagination. But despite the certainty of my mind, my soul held out hope.

By 10:00 p.m., still holding onto hope, my soul convinced mind and body to try something new. "I've spent all day waiting for Joy to arrive," it whispered. "I haven't done anything to make Joy happen. I can help create what I want. I can manifest Joy's arrival myself," it announced.

"But how?" I listened for the intuition that is the voice of the soul, and it was then I heard it whisper, "Just sit for a few moments, and see what comes to mind."

In minutes, I was smiling at the fruit of my efforts. Of course! I had never asked Joy to come! I had spent all day waiting for her arrival, but I had never made a declaration to myself and her that I wanted her here. If I want her to come, then perhaps the best place to start is with an invitation.

I sat in silence for a moment, and then, with all the resolve I could muster, declared aloud, "Joy, I want you here. No conditions. No limits. No restrictions. Teach me."

Suddenly, there was a knock at the door. I knew in moments the adventure would be underway.

Chapter 11

The Night of Infinite Possibility

I hurried down the stairs and threw open the door. There she was, radiant as ever, a shining star on a cold, dark winter's night.

"Come," she said, "you've waited long enough."

I nodded my head in exaggerated fashion, my body language sharing an overstated, "Yes, I have." I took a deep breath, released a sigh, and shared an exasperated, "I've been waiting all day." I hoped she'd be impressed by my dedication.

She looked at me oddly, as if I had completely misunderstood. It occurred to me then that perhaps everything she spoke had meaning as deep as the ocean, and all I kept hearing and responding to were the waves on the surface. A thought jumped me, distracting me. "A metaphor for your life," it declared.

"No," she responded, jolting me back to her presence, "you have not only been waiting all day, you have waited a lifetime to give yourself this journey. It has always been available to you, but it is only now that you have made yourself ready."

"Oh," I said, my tone revealing the disappointment that I had not journeyed this way sooner. "Why didn't I create this years ago?" I asked, indicting myself with a pointed question from my inner critic.

"Sweet one," she said gently, seeing my self-incrimination expressed outwardly through my abrupt change in body language, "do not regret the past, nor judge it. It is that which you cannot change. All that is left is to learn from it, and live those learnings now."

It was as if those words reminded her of an urgency about her time here tonight. She walked in the doorway, taking me by the hand. I was elated by the touch of our hands, and as we walked up the stairs, I dulled my other senses, enhancing my delight in the warmth of her softness.

She lay down in the middle of the living room floor, and tugged on my hand, motioning for me to lie down beside her. When I did, she invited me to close my eyes.

"I want you to focus on your breath," she shared, an irresistible blend of gentleness and confidence in her voice. "And as a way to help you do that, I want you to take a few deep breaths." She began to speak in rhythm to my breathing. "Inhaling deeply...and letting go...inhaling deeply...and letting go...inhaling deeply...and letting go."

"Excellent," she shared in reward. "Now, allow your breath to return to its own gentle, easy rhythms. Focus on the rising and falling of your lungs with each breath. Filling up...and letting go...filling up...and letting go...filling up...and letting go."

"Wonderful," she declared. "Now, to the feelings of lungs filling and releasing, add the sensation of air flowing gently in through your nostrils, and down along your windpipe, filling your lungs ... and as you exhale, feel the flow of air outward, from lungs, through windpipe, and out through the nostrils."

"Magnificent," she announced, continuing her encouragement through praise. "Finally, feel the rising of your stomach as your lungs fill with sweet precious air, the gift of life, and feel the falling of your stomach as your lungs release, preparing themselves for a new breath."

It was strange to suddenly experience sensations that had been taking place in my body my whole life. Stranger still was how relaxing it was. "Was peace so close at hand that all I had to do to achieve it was grow an awareness of my breathing?" I pondered inwardly. A stranger question came my way then: "Had the Universe given humankind a gift, the gift of breath, as a simple way to always experience the peace within, if only they would focus on its gentle, calming rhythm?"

"Yes, to both your questions," I heard a voice say. I couldn't tell if it was Joy or imagined words from deep within. Somehow, in that moment, it didn't seem to matter.

I remembered the story Joy had told me, of a King who had

wanted to know love in a new way. In the story, he had hid the Love he was inside of him, and created a world around him that insisted Love was found on the outside. "Perhaps that King," I pondered, adding my own chapter to his story, "overwhelmed by the task he had created for himself, gave himself the gift of breath, so that he could in any moment remember the breath, and in doing so, open the doorway to the wonder within."

"Come back to your breathing," I heard Joy announce, breaking through my cloud of thoughts. "In...out...in...out...in...out." Her voice was mesmerizing, and in a moment I returned to the experience of my breath.

"Nowhere to go...and nothing to do. You have nowhere to go ...and nothing to do. Just be here now in the fullness of this moment. Just be here now in the wonder of this moment...in the fullness and wonder of this breath." Through her words, my shoulders relaxed and my body eased. It was as if each cell had breathed its own sigh of relief. It was as if, somehow, there had never been anywhere to go, nor anything to do, ever.

"Now, allow yourself to sink into an easy, gentle space inside," she continued. "Feel inside of you a space, deep down...a place of unreasonable compassion...a home of unbounded love. Feel it there inside you, a wondrous, joyous space, calling you, summoning you...come...come home at last.

"Let yourself sink deep...then deeper...and deeper, moving closer and closer to that space inside of you. Feel yourself drop downward, gently floating down into that easy, gentle place inside.

"Beautiful," she continued. "Let yourself drop deeper still...and even deeper now, moving slowly...and gently...to the most nurturing, compassionate space inside of you.

"And, as you float downward...allow yourself to look up, and, with your mind's eye, notice around you a night sky ...beautiful, glorious night sky...stars dancing with delight...stars winking at their wonder."

I saw it now, as clearly as I had ever seen anything before: a glorious night sky, a million stars above, each one warm and inviting, and me floating in the midst of it all, as calm and relaxed as ever in my life.

And then, there she was, beside me, shining more brightly than any star in the sky, my Joy. She smiled at me, and I felt then that this was one of the most glorious moments of my life.

"It is the Night of Infinite Possibility," she declared. "Every star in the sky is a journey, a journey to a different place, and a different time. You are always free to come here," she welcomed, "anytime you choose. This is a place and a time created by the Divine, the Divine in You, to help you see what you once missed, to empower you to learn whatever it is you choose."

I was overwhelmed by the beauty of this place, its magnificence, and the feeling of total acceptance that surrounded me here. It was a feeling I had waited for all my life, fearing I would only experience it in death. And yet here I was, touching the experience, feeling more alive than ever before.

Thoughts crept in, attempting to sabotage the perfection of the moment. "Are you worthy of this experience?" one cried out. "What have you done in your life to deserve such bliss?" another demanded. "Who are you to be rewarded with even a moment of such incredible wonder?" a third interrogated. "This is some sort of mistake," my thoughts decided in unanimity, "as if somehow the mail had been delivered to the wrong house, only this time it wasn't mail, it was Joy."

"Funny," a new thought piped in, "you waited your whole life to get to a place like this, and in the moment you're here, all you can think about is how you don't truly deserve to be here."

"And that," Joy announced with supreme confidence, responding to the thoughts of my mind, "is why you have never come here before."

Joy's words broke the downward spiral of my earlier thoughts. New ones came to me, this time inspired by the beauty of this place. They filled me with sudden gratitude, which quickly grew beyond words. I tried words anyway.

"Thank you, so much, for bringing me here," I announced.

My feelings of thankfulness, for knowing even a moment in a place as abundant as this, were beginning to overwhelm me. My pleasure in being here grew so great so fast, it was overwhelming, and I could no longer contain my feelings in the limiting space of my body. Tears began their journey down the length of my face. Tears of gratitude. Tears of thanks. Tears that said, "Home at last!"

"Come," Joy announced, gently placing my hand in hers. "We have much to do on this night." Hand in hand, we floated upward into the star-filled sky, moving slowly toward the infinite expanse of sparkling gems illuminating the dark.

"Which one?" Joy inquired.

"Which one what?"

"Which star would you like to travel to tonight?"

They all looked beautiful to me. "I don't know," I announced.

"Sweet one," Joy responded softly, "you do know. You have always known that which was perfect for you. You have just forgotten how to listen."

"Use the wisdom of heart and soul. Feel your way."

It sounded wonderful, but I had no idea how to do it. "How?"

She looked at me, an expression revealing a little surprise, but its softness showing great patience. "In this moment, look in the night sky," she said softly, guiding me gently. She waited for me to turn and look upward.

"Now," she continued, "ask yourself which one feels right."

The words and the way she spoke were music to my soul, as if it had waited years for this permission to guide. But my mind protested. If I was going to lead myself through this journey tonight, it wanted detailed instruction.

"How do I decide which feels right?" I spoke, acquiescing to the demands of my mind.

"Close your eyes." She waited while I fulfilled her request. "Now, when I ask you to open them, look at the expanse of night sky before you. In that first moment of vision, see what star welcomes you, and guide us there. Do not question your decision in the moments after you make it. Do not ask whether your chosen star shines more brightly than that one, and maybe we should be following her brighter sister. Do not think this star is prettier in shape than yours, and perhaps we should be guided by the star with the heart-like shape. Simply see, in that first moment of looking, who calls to you."

"Now, open your eyes."

I looked heavenward at the vision of perfection that lay before me, and there she was, my star, signaling to me with her twinkling. My mind wanted to protest, declare that this was no way to decide, but then I remembered Joy's words, and released all indecision that followed that first moment. "I've got it," I announced proudly.

"Wonderful," she shared. Hand in hand we floated upward toward the smallest of shinings in a night aglow with starlight.

We drifted higher and higher into the heavens, gliding with the greatest of ease through the expanse of night sky. The closer we moved to the star that called to me, the larger it grew, until it was no longer a star, but a soft light, inviting us to enter into its warm embrace. I followed its call, Joy's hand in mine, and soon the light grew to such brightness that it dwarfed the night sky.

Seeking the embrace of its gentleness, wanting the welcome of its softness, I entered into the light, Joy by my side.

As I floated in the embrace of the light, I felt that this was no ordinary light, but rather a light destined to take us on a journey, a fantastic journey through space and time. I didn't believe it at first, but there they were, drifting by as we moved through the warmth. Numbers. No. Years. Yes. Years drifting by. "1991" floated its way past us, with "1990" on its heals. The eighties came next, number after number moving its way past us, faster and faster. We were accelerating on our journey. The seventies were a blur, but with the coming of "1970," the numbers slowed dramatically. "1969" was slow in coming. "1968" crawled its way into sight. The end of the light was near.

As gently as we had glided into the light, we floated our way out. For a moment there was darkness, and then I saw her.

Chapter 12

Birth

There, right in front of me, the face of a woman. She looked undeniably familiar, and yet I couldn't quite place her.

Before I could speak, her face convulsed, as if suddenly in excruciating pain. Her mouth opened in anguish, then her teeth clenched in agony. A moan of distress escaped her lips. "Help me," she cried out, the pain reflected in her tone. Something was wrong here, terribly wrong.

"Joy, what's happening?" I said hurriedly, almost panicked, my mind rushing to find a way to save this woman from whatever crisis she might be encountering.

Joy turned to me, amused in the midst of my panic, as if somehow I had once again seen only a glimmer of the whole, and in so doing misunderstood the world around me. "Look around," she said. "See where you are before deciding what you are to do here."

I pulled my vision back from the woman's face, my mind still trying to place her. She looked strikingly familiar, yet somehow different enough that she escaped my memory. I broke away from the vision of her, viewing the room that surrounded me for the first time.

The woman I was seeing lay uncomfortably on a bed with a metal frame. She was dressed in a plain white robe...a hospital robe? There was something very strange about her belly, the way it jutted out. Her legs were raised, and a single white sheet covered them. Beside her was a man, also unmistakably familiar, but inexplicably unrecognizable. He was holding her hand with great care, a look of grave concern painting his face. I turned to the foot of bed, seeking the source of new sounds coming from behind the woman's raised, covered legs. There, seated, was a nurse, and beside her in an unmistakable white mask, a doctor. In moments, my mind pieced together the patchwork of imagery sent its way by my vision. This was the miracle of birth.

It occurred to me then that these people, woman, man, nurse, and doctor alike, were strangely oblivious to the sudden appearance of Joy and me.

"They can neither see nor hear us. While we may experience them, they have no experience of us," Joy explained, responding to the thoughts of my mind.

"Then...why are we here?"

"All things in the fullness of time," she replied. "Just wait, watch, and hang on to your socks. All things will become clear soon enough."

I turned my attention to the woman's face, deciding that I would once again try to place her. As I studied her features, her face relaxed for a moment, then convulsed again, her neck twitching backward in sync with the coming wave of pain.

"Push," announced the man by her side, a weak attempt at encouragement.

She had little energy to speak, but his words seemed to frustrate her so that despite her situation she mustered the energy to respond, "What <huff> the hell <huff> do you think <huff> I'm doing?"

"I'm just trying to help, Mary," he offered, defensively.

Mary? Had he said Mary? Mary? But...Mary was my Mom's name. Mom?

"Mom? Mom!" I shouted, suddenly realizing why she had looked so familiar, and yet somehow unknowable. This was my Mom, years into the past. And...

"Dad? Dad! Dad! It's me." There was no denying it, this was Mom and that was Dad by her side.

I was so excited at the prospect of seeing them, and so very much wanting them to see me, that I shouted loudly, "Mom! Dad! It's me!"

The sounds of silence in response quickly reminded me of my current state of existence.

But if this was Mom, and that was Dad, and it was 1968, and they were about to have a child...no way! My mind wasn't ready to believe the inevitable conclusion presented by the facts at hand. I wanted some external confirmation.

"Joy, is this *my* birth?"

She looked at me, her expression speaking more clearly than words: you don't need my answer to validate what you already know is true.

I was jolted back to the room by Mom's moan of agony, louder now than the ones before. Something was happening, and it was something big. I could feel the energy Mom exerted growing ten-fold.

What was happening?

"I see a head," a voice from the foot of the bed announced triumphantly, as if responding to my question.

"C'mon Mary, you're almost there. Just one more..." Dad started, only to be interrupted.

"Shut <huff> up <huff> or <huff> I < huff> swear <huff> I'll stop <huff> right <huff> here <huff> and <huff> leave <huff> <huff> right <huff> now."

Poor Dad, I thought. He was quiet after that, and the sounds of the room were overtaken by the moans and grunts of Mom pushing herself beyond exhaustion, beyond her threshold of pain. Her face contorted beyond recognition, her body convulsed, as if thrusting toward a giant orgasm. And then, without warning, she stopped.

"I've got him," came the voice from the foot of the bed. "A beautiful baby boy."

A silence filled the room, as if somehow the miracle of the moment was beyond the description of spoken word. Dad's eyes told tales of pride and love, Mom's were a mix of awe and utter exhaustion.

The silence was broken by the scream of the newborn, his response to a sudden slap on the rear. "Quite a welcome," one of my thoughts announced. "Well, best to warn him what it's like in the real world sooner than later," another jumped in. "That's the first of many sudden slaps he'll get in his life," yet another thought piped out.

My train of thinking was suddenly derailed by the scene unfolding before my eyes.

The little man was delivered, blood, tears, goo and all, into the arms of Mom. Her face transformed into a radiant glow, and the exhaustion of moments ago vanished without trace. She held him in her arms with such gentleness and warmth that it must have seemed to him that he had returned to the safety of the womb, for in her arms, he stopped his crying.

Comforted by her unconditional love, he returned her glance, and it seemed to me as if his eyes spoke a gentle thank you.

The moment my eyes caught the newborn's, I was mesmerized by the miracle of his new life. Big blue eyes experienced the world with neither judgment nor condemnation, seeking instead to capture the fullness of the moment. His nose was barely visible, just a thin outline dotted with two small nostrils. His lips were a thin trace around an open mouth, revealing soft pink gums void of the teeth that would come with age. His face was round, his cheeks full.

And then I remembered, where I was, who this was I was looking at...me! This was me! This is me! This is my Birth!

"Boy, kid, you'd better enjoy that cute little nose while you've got it, because it's going to outgrow your other facial features before you reach puberty," one thought announced. "And enjoy that hair while you've got it, too, because that receding line your granddad has, well, it's contagious," another declared.

But there was something more profound going on here. I could hear my soul inviting my mind to know quiet, so I could experience the something bigger that I had journeyed all this way to learn. My mind acquiesced, and I sat in silence, looking at the tiny new me before me.

As I embraced him with my eyes, I was overwhelmed by his perfection. "This tiny reflection of humanity is perfect just as he is," I announced inwardly. "If he never changes one iota from where he is right now, it is okay. He is, already, perfection."

Next, I saw his Divinity. "This is a child of God. As clearly as I see his features, I see now the God in him," I declared. "In these early moments of life, he is Buddha, Christ and Mohammed. He is living through God, just as God is living through him. I see the King from Joy's story alive in his presence."

I could feel his undeniable belief in self, and, as an outgrowth, an unflappable faith in the universe around him. "He knows nothing *but* to believe in himself. He trusts himself to cry when he feels it necessary, and trusts himself to smile when he chooses, never thinking 'maybe this is not right' or 'this not appropriate.' He never censors the splendor of who he is—he just lives it.

"He has absolute faith in everything and everyone around him, an outgrowth of the faith he has in himself. In a world that is a hostile, violent place, he knows only to trust it with his life. In return, the world around him bends, changing its state of reality, responding to show him that his trust will be rewarded."

And that *was me*. Years ago.

"No," Joy's voice came from the back of the room, "that is you, now. It is who you truly are, but you refuse to see yourself in that way."

I wanted to speak to her, ask her what she meant, but it was as if her words triggered an explosion of new thoughts in me. I wanted them heard before I returned my attention to Joy. The flurry of thoughts in my mind organized themselves quickly, and weaved themselves into this:

Once upon a time, there was born unto this planet, a creature so divine that to see him was to see Love. He was so perfect, that in his moment of birth no one wanted to change him in any way, ever. For his perfection was a joy to behold.

 The little creature believed in himself, in his place in the world, and in the world around him. Never once did he doubt the wonder of who he was, nor the wonder of the world around him. He never questioned why he was here. He knew it was all as it should be.

Born completely helpless, he did not protest about the injustice of his condition, nor complain about how he lacked the defenses to protect himself from harm. Instead, he decided if this was where he was, then he would delight in it fully, and trust the universe to care for him. His trust was a miracle to those around him, and a great teacher to those who chose to listen.

Most of all, he was the King of the Kingdom of the Soul. To see him was to see God, for God lived in him just as surely as he lived in God.

Many years later, the exact same being, only bigger now in size, looks at himself. He calls himself terrible and awful. He berates himself when he does not succeed in creating what he wants. He roots himself in the belief that he is not perfect.

He does not trust the world nor his place in it. Whenever he is denied what he wants, he screams at the universe regarding the injustice of it all.

He doubts that God exists, never mind that he is living God, just as God is living him.

What has changed? Has in fact the very same creature, in the years since his birth, lost his perfection, lost his Divinity? Are these things that can be lost?

NO! These things are gifts of grace from the Universe, and they are not for him to lose!

What has changed then, for this creature?

He has forgotten!

It is not that he is no longer perfect. He can never lose the perfection of who he is. All that has changed is that he has forgotten his perfection.

It is not that he is no longer trustworthy. He cannot lose that. He has merely forgotten his trustworthiness.

It is not that he is no longer Divine. That is not his to lose. What has changed is that he has forgotten his Divinity.

You are the perfection, the trust, the Divinity of the newborn who now sits in front of you. What you see before you is you, and all that you see in him lives in you now, if only you would dare to remember! What you see, and all the wisdom you see, in him, is in you, here and now, all these years later. If only you would believe!

"But how did I forget?" I wondered. "These are the most important things in life to remember."

"That is for another journey." Joy's words interrupted my thinking. "Come, our time here is done. It is time for us to take leave."

I offered no protest, overwhelmed by the events of the previous moments, my mind still reeling from the revelations of my soul.

Hand in hand, we lifted off the floor, floated through the room, out the hospital window, and up into a night sky. Immediately, I saw her again, waiting patiently for us, winking at us to ensure we would not miss our ride home—my sweet friend, the traveling star. As we moved toward her, she shared the brilliance of her light with us a second time. We welcomed the embrace of her warmth and her comfort as her light surrounded us.

Again, we journeyed through her, down the passageways of time. Years floated by in their usual sequence, "1968" first, the present year last. With the coming of today, came the end of our journey through the tunnel of light.

We emerged from the brightness. I, expecting a return to the Night of Infinite Possibilities, was surprised to experience the gentle rhythms of my breath, as it filled and released, filled and released. I felt the hardness of the living room floor beneath me. We were back, back in our bodies, back in my home.

Slowly, I moved my fingers and my toes, wanting my return to the physical realm to be a gradual reentry. Soon, I was turning my wrists and ankles, then moving entire legs and arms. Finally, I opened my eyes.

"Joy?" I questioned, surprised to find her gone from the floor beside me. I rose slowly, then looked through the house. She had disappeared as mysteriously as she arrived. A part of me knew beyond doubt that she would be back next Saturday, not one to break a promise.

Exhausted, I stumbled my way to bed, and fell into deep sleep.

Chapter 13

Guilty Verdict

I knew when I awoke the next morning that everything would be exactly the same, yet inexplicably different. I had the seen the magnificence of Who I Really Am. I could feel the perfection of a newborn alive in me. His Divinity was my birthright.

While my soul felt newfound wonder, my mind began to deny it. It argued against the possibility.

"Who are you to think that you are so wonderful?" one thought insisted. "Who are you to think yourself perfect?" another piped out. "Who are you to think that God is alive in you, and you alive in God?" another shouted, demanding an answer.

"Who are you *not* to think these things are true?" a soft soul-thought offered in reply.

Angry thoughts were enraged by the question. "What kind of answer is that?" they shot back. They gathered together, mounting a barbaric offensive.

"Sure, you may have started this life in innocence, you may have started out rooted in the Divine, maybe you even started out perfect...but look what you've done with it!" my thoughts began, presenting their case. Next came a collection of evidence gathered from throughout my life, supporting claims of imperfection.

"Exhibit A," a thought announced, pointing to imaginary evidence, "your sister's doll. Note the purple mustache you painted across it."

"Exhibit B, your honor," another continued, "a broken promise. You swore on your life, to yourself and your parents, that you would never go to that arcade again, but where were you the very next day?"

A third thought spoke out: "Exhibit C, pornographic material—need I say more?

"Exhibit D—traffic and the way you drive through it, cutting off drivers and raging at those who cut you off."

By the time my thoughts made it through the alphabet, the evidence was overwhelming. A guilty verdict was all any sane jury could hand down. "Where was your perfection then? Where is your Divinity now?" my thoughts announced, presenting their two-question closing argument.

I had no idea. The evidence seemed undeniable.

If I couldn't lose perfection, I sure did a good job of hiding it from myself in that moment.

If I couldn't lose Divinity, then I sure did outstanding work convincing myself it was lost.

If I couldn't lose the wonder of who I am, I found a way to bury it alive under the boulders of judgment.

Yet, somewhere, deep inside, despite my collection of incriminating evidence and the self-inflicted guilty verdict, a part of me had seen my glory in the eyes of the newborn that I once was. I held out hope that somewhere, down deep, I was still the brilliance of that little God I had seen last night.

I wanted so much more than to just hold out hope for my brilliance. I wanted to *know.* Who was I, really? If I was the perfection I saw last night, then what of the misery I had caused in the world around me? How did I explain that? If I was perfection, why was I in this place of deep unhappiness? And...how do I get out?

Saturday

January 26

Chapter 14

The Ambassador of the Soul

A new Saturday dawned, filling me with hope and promise.

"What would you like to learn today with Joy?" an inquisitive thought piped out in my early waking moments.

My mind raced through the infinite possibilities of things known and unknowable. Some thoughts argued I should learn *this*, others were convinced I should figure *that* out. It wasn't long before I realized that my mind was no place to look for an answer only a soul could provide.

To get in touch with soul, I lay down on the floor, closed my eyes and focused on my breath. I used remembered words from my time with Joy as my guide.

Breathing deeply three times, I then let my breath return to its own easy natural rhythm.

I felt the filling up and release of the lungs. I imagined them now as the beat of the breath, my inner rhythmic drummer.

I experienced the rush of air through my nostrils and down my windpipe. I imagined this as my internal flute.

Next, the rising and falling of stomach was transformed into the puffing cheeks of my internal trumpet player. Soon, I fell deeply into the experience of the internal orchestra that was my breath.

There, before me, in the calmness of this internal space, words walked upward from a deep place within, climbing their way into my mind. I read the words as they reached their destination.

> Once, there lived a being. His birthright was love and joy beyond measure.
>
> As the being grew, he formed a mind, a tool to help him in the journey of life.
>
> But in his mind, he forgot his birthright.
>
> Indeed, in his mind he more than forgot. His mind collected evidence to support a new, misguided belief, a belief in that which he was not. His mind convinced the being that down deep there was something wrong with him.
>
> His mind argued that he was, in some unknowable way, fundamentally flawed. The being believed the words of a mind lost in unhappy thoughts.

The being's life, as a consequence, became an experience in naught but fear and distress.

Then, one day, the being declared that he had had enough of the experience of misery that his mind had created. He was ready for something more.

His soul said, "At last."

It sent an ambassador to help the being find his way out of the false constructs of his mind, and bring him back home to the wisdom which was his birthright.

First, the Ambassador of the Soul took the being to the truth of his existence, in a way that let him see, undeniably, who he really was.

But the being's mind was strong, for it had lived a whole life convinced of its misguided beliefs. It would not be so easily thwarted from its way.

"Change is far more risky than a tolerable level of unhappiness," the mind argued. With those words, it mounted a brutal offensive.

The soul, in its infinite patience, sent its ambassador back for a second time, for a second learning, one that would soothe the raging tides of a mind on the offensive.

"How nice that you have brought yourself here," came a voice, soft as a gentle breeze, brimming with the confidence of a dawning sun. "We can move more easily to our next journey from here."

"Joy!" I exclaimed, unable to contain the excitement that her presence instilled in me. "I am so glad to see you!"

"As I am glad to see you, dear one," she offered. "And it is splendid to find you listening to the music of your inner world. Her rhythms will one day lead you to the peace that has eluded you all these years."

Joy's words were reassuring. After a week of mind battling soul, it was wonderful to have someone offer such positive affirmation with such unflappable confidence.

"Joy, are you the ambassador of my soul?" I asked, linking her presence to my soul story.

The warmth of her smile was the only response she offered.

"Come," she said, "from here it is only a short journey to the Night of Infinite Possibility." She took me by my hand, and together we floated deeper into my internal world.

In moments, we stopped, I looking up into a night sky filled with as many stars as there were possibilities.

"Where to tonight?" Joy asked.

"How should I..." I interrupted my words, suddenly remembering exactly how I should. I closed my eyes, stilled my thoughts, and then opened my eyes wide. In that first moment, I saw her, as clearly as I'd ever seen anything before. A star, much bigger than the last, calling to me, inviting me to travel to her world of possibility.

"This way," I said, taking Joy by the hand.

Chapter 15

Illusions

We glided upward toward the star, and she grew in greeting, transforming herself into a warm glow, soon dwarfing the night sky. I entered into her confidently, surrounding myself with her brilliance, Joy by my side. I was filled with excitement, remembering with delight the birth I experienced on my previous journey.

The light embraced us, welcoming us on our next voyage. As we traveled through her, I could feel the flow of months, then the reversal of the years. When the light presented us with its end, I knew we had arrived at our destination: 1971.

In the moments after my emergence from the light, there was darkness. But my eyes were quicker to adjust this time than last, and quickly they were taking in my new surroundings.

I was sitting, cramped, in the back seat of a 1968 VW Bug. To my right was Joy, squashed into the small space afforded her by this tiny car. On my left, with legroom to spare, was a three-year-old, sitting happily, rocking his legs back and forth to the rhythm of an imagined song. Beside him were two large brown grocery bags, each one overflowing, the head of a solitary baguette protruding proudly from one of them.

In front of us sat a man and a woman, deeply engaged in conversation. The man, driving, was speaking.

"Mary," he announced, "I can't believe how little we can get for $20 these days."

"I know," she concurred. "Used to be we could get so much more."

I recognized that brief conversation, the words spoken and the way they were said. That was Dad driving, engaging Mom in familiar dialogue.

The little man to my right, then, content with the world around him, happily engaging in imaginary songs, was me, aged three.

Suddenly, as if responding to an unseen grumbling in his stomach, Little Me grabbed ahold of a grocery bag, pulled it toward him with great effort, then peered into its top. He looked with great interest, eyes open wide, a quest for a little something to soothe the calls of hunger. Nothing in the bag of worth, he must have thought as he pushed it away. He leaned over its top, continuing his search in the neighboring bag.

His eyes lit with excitement when he saw it. He couldn't believe his good fortune. There, peering out of the bag, the tip of a fresh baguette.

He touched it, and was delighted to discover it still hot. He tore off its top end with relish, throwing it quickly to his side.

He sank his hand into its soft white interior, his eyes dancing with excitement. In moments his hand emerged, victorious, filled with all of the insides that his tiny fingers could pull out.

He placed his handful of fresh dough into his mouth with great joy, as if a ravenous king suddenly offered a feast. It must have tasted as wonderful as he had imagined, because before finishing his first bite, his hand reached into the baguette for more.

In moments, he had tunneled a hole through its center, scooping its interior out, one little handful at a time.

It was in that last incriminating moment, one final piece of fluffy white interior in one hand, a hollow baguette in the other, that Mom turned to see how her son was doing.

To my surprise, he smiled at her, excitedly showing her this new and most delicious way he himself had uncovered to satisfy the cries of his stomach. But Mom didn't see the scene with the same eyes of joyful discovery.

"How could you?" she said, more indictment than question. She raised her tone. "I can't believe you just did this! What will we serve the guests tonight?" She shook her head, disapprovingly, and while she never spoke the words, her body language shouted them. "You're a bad boy. A very bad boy."

The joy Little Me had been experiencing, the fun of song, the triumph of discovery, the wonder of great taste, vanished in those moments of incrimination. He sat back quietly, tentative and unsure.

"That is what we have come to see," announced Joy, the gravity of her tone suggesting we had just seen an act of great significance.

"That? Me burrowing my way through a loaf of fresh bread, Mom stopping me. I came all this way to see *that?*" There was no hiding the disappointment echoing in my words.

"Yes, but there is far, far more here than meets your eye. There are, in these moments witnessed, answers to questions you have been asking for years."

"Answers to what questions?"

"Rather than have me tell you, why not see for yourself," she stated, handing me a pair of rose-colored glasses.

"You've got to be kidding. You want me to see the world through rose-colored glasses? You know," I declared, repeating a saying I'd heard a thousand times before, "you can't see the world through rose-colored glasses."

"My sweet friend," Joy replied, "there is simply no better way."

I put on the glasses, and suddenly the world was alive with

color and light. As I looked around, I saw not only the external world, but internal worlds as well.

I looked at the little man to my left, sitting solemnly. I could see and feel the colored energy emanating from his body and the thoughts spoken only in his mind. Together, they were my gateway into his entire universe of the moment:

> I was moving through the world, exploring it and experiencing it in the very best way I knew how. When Mom and Dad are hungry, I see how they search for food to eat and, when they find something that excites them, they eat it. Hadn't I done the very same thing? I was only doing what I had been taught to do by their example.
>
> Why was I yelled at?

He searched for answers in his mind, over and over again. He searched all the possibilities he could imagine. Finally, there was but one left in his little mind.

> I moved through the world in the best way I knew how. I did my very best to take care of myself. And yet, even seeing all this, Mom turned and when she saw me, she saw me as bad. And Mom knows. Mom knows best. Well, if Mom called me bad, then I must be...

"Oh, no!" I said inwardly, feelings of dread creeping up my spine, "Don't say it! Don't say it!" He said it anyway, despite my internal pleas.

> ...bad. I must be bad. There must be something wrong with me. Here I am enjoying the fullness of

life, and Mom turns to me and her body language shouts BAD! She must be right. There's something wrong with me. I can't quite place what it is. But if Mom sees it, it must be there.

So that's how it started, my belief in my badness. It was Mom's fault. I looked at Mom, furious for all the years of suffering her careless act was going to cause that Little Me. But when I saw her through the rose-colored glasses, my anger dissipated in the clarity of newfound insight. Through my glasses, I could see her invisible world of energy and thought.

I told him to wait until we got home. We'd feed him then. I even enticed him by offering his favorite. He agreed. And there he was eating the bread.

Now what will I serve the guests coming over tonight? I can't very well serve them hollowed out bread. And there isn't the time to go back to the store and still prepare for the guests. Damn.

I hate yelling at him, I hate the way I feel inside when I do it, but sometimes it just seems like the quickest, fastest way to get him to stop. It's a fast, easy way to get him to stop doing the things I don't want him to do.

Mom felt guilty yelling at her only son. She justified her shouting, explaining to herself why she had done it, hoping to cut short her remorse before it grew inside her.

I yell because he stops when I do. By screaming at him, he understands how much I want him to stop. Shouting motivates him, more than anything else I can think of. It gets quick results and stops unwanted behaviors. It's the very best I can do.

I could stop and explain to him that he's doing things I don't want, and what he could do differently...but who has that kind of time? No, Mary, you can't expect yourself to explain every time your son does something you don't want. You'd spend all day explaining.

Yelling gets you what you want: he stops. And he understands, I'm sure, that you just want him to stop.

"You've got to be kidding me," I declared inwardly. "Mom is also just doing the best she can. Then that means...no way!"

But the conclusion was inevitable.

"Joy," I said, seeking external confirmation for what I now knew was true, "my belief that down deep there must be something wrong with me...my belief that I am not perfect just the way I am...is based on a misunderstanding?"

Joy looked at me, her eyes inviting me to answer my own question.

"I started to believe that there must be something wrong with me when my parents started yelling at me, telling me to stop whatever it was I was doing—painting the walls with watercolors, testing out new crayons in Mom's magazines, making rivers of juice on the rug.

"All I was doing was delighting in the world, and suddenly I saw the world stop delighting in me. I took my parents words and body language literally, when they called me bad. I began in those moments to believe in my badness.

"But they never meant it that way. All they were saying was 'we want you to stop what you're doing,' and this was the best way they knew to get results.

"No one ever meant to tell me there was something wrong with me...I decided I was bad...based on a misunderstanding."

"Of course, dear one," Joy replied, "how else could it be? You are, truly, perfection. You are wondrous just as you are, if only you could see yourself as I see you. I see the oceans of beauty that hide beneath the thin dams of fear that you have built for yourself over your entire life."

"Joy," I said, "I'm...beautiful? I just misunderstood."

"Of course, dear sweet friend. You have simply chosen a belief that hides the very truth of Who You Are from you."

Thoughts mugged me, coming by the hundreds, overwhelming my mind. When at last I pieced them together, they shared their story with me.

> Once there was born a wondrous being, so beautiful that to see him was to love him. He hid nothing of himself, neither his perfection, nor his Divinity, nor his trust of himself and of the world around him.
>
> As the being grew, he explored the world in new and exciting ways. First, he learned to crawl his way through it. Soon, the time came when he rose on his hind legs and walked through the world around him, much like the giants he shared his home with.

The being wanted nothing more than to experience the world fully. He felt it, touched it, smelled it, heard it and, most of all, tasted it. How he loved to taste the world, putting everything he could find in his mouth for exploration.

But, strangely, at what seemed like random moments to him, giants ran in from time to time, interjecting, screaming, "Bad, bad boy!" The energy behind their words spoke far more forcefully than the words themselves.

The little being was puzzled by these violent appearances. What did they mean?

One year left, giving birth to the one thereafter. The sudden appearances of angry giants, now with names (Mom and Dad) grew in frequency.

The little creature searched for the source of their anger. He thought perhaps it was something he was doing, so he tried to change his behavior. But then the giants simply found some other reason to yell. The cause of the anger couldn't be something outside of him, he declared, it must be something in him.

In a moment, he made a decision, a decision that changed his mind in a way that would change his life. "It must be me. There must be something wrong with me. Down deep, I am broken. Built with a missing part. It is the only way to explain why the big people see the wrong in me with such regularity."

And so the being, despite his birthright, which was perfection, Divinity, and trust, abandoned these parts of himself.

The being collected mountains of evidence to confirm his badness, and buried his birthright under his mountains.

It was his mountain to build. It would be his to remove. Down deep, the being knew, "There is nothing to do in this life but move the mountain, one rock at a time. Then, I shall shine the wonder of who I really am for the world to see."

"Now," said Joy, "you understand. You see how you lost your belief in the perfection that is and always will be you."

"Yes," I announced, "now I understand."

"Understanding is the first step," Joy responded. "Experiencing what you understand will be the next."

Without a word spoken between us, I knew that our time here was compete. Joy and I floated upward, through the window of the VW Bug, and up into the evening sky. It was winter, and the sky had already turned to darkness, revealing the brilliance of her stars. I recognized the one that had brought us here immediately, and floated, hand in hand with Joy, toward her welcome embrace.

The star transformed herself as we moved toward her, lighting up the night sky with her warm glow. We entered into her, surrounding ourselves with the softness and the love of her caress. She took us through the tunnel way of time, returning me to the place I had called home for the last few months. When I emerged from the light, I felt the gentle rhythms of my breath, and the harshness of the floor beneath my body.

Again, I awoke gently from my journey, moving fingers and toes, growing into the motion of ankles and wrists, and then entire arms and legs moved. At last, I slowly opened my eyes.

I expected to find no Joy, imagining her gone without a trace of her ever being here, just as she had the time before. Much to my surprise, my open eyes found Joy aglow in my living room, a vision of beauty on my couch.

"This week, sweet one," she announced, "I will ask something of you. You have been blessed with a vision of the wonder that you are. You have heard how, through misunderstanding, you have created an illusion of that which you are not.

"It is time to shift from hearing to experiencing. For it is said that to hear is to understand, but to experience is to *know*. And I want you to *know* the fullness of who it is that you really are.

"So here is what I ask of you.

"You, in your lifetime, have collected evidence to support what you believe about yourself," Joy began. "You have, for so many years, believed in your badness, that you have attics filled with files of incrimination. You have libraries filled with evidence of how imperfect you really are.

"I tell you now: It is time for something new!" She spoke now with great passion and conviction. "Begin to collect evidence to support a new belief: You are wondrous beyond even your wildest of imaginings. You are Divine, an expression of Divinity. Go this week, and be a lawyer in your own defense.

Gather up every shred of evidence, from everything you do this week, to support a belief in the new, perfect you."

I had never heard Joy speak with such determination. I was swept up in her tide of words, adrift in the sea of wonder that her words spun in my mind.

"Yes!" I said resoundingly. "I'll do it."

"Thank you," she replied gently. With that, she arose from the couch, flowed with grace and ease to the entrance way stairs, and let herself out.

I sat, mesmerized by the journey left behind, and excited by the one to come.

Chapter 16

Trials by Fire

It's amazing to me how the excitement and enthusiasm of one moment can be so quickly surrendered to the next. I started the week with what I felt was unflappable determination to collect evidence surrounding my perfection.

Each morning began with a reaffirmation. I welcomed the day with the promise of hope and the vastness of possibility. But, usually sooner than later, I forgot my promise to show myself my wonder. I returned to a lifetime of practiced unhappiness.

Some days, in the frenetic nature of my morning drive, I traded in collecting evidence of perfection for moments of shared anger with a neighboring driver.

Other days, I found examples of my magnificence all the way to work. But, once there, I forgot my commitment to myself and my Joy in the job-of-the-moment. I hurried through work, trading in visions of perfection for old patterns of judgment and indictment.

Each day, I eventually remembered my commitment to collect evidence in support of my perfection. But by the time memory returned, it was too late.

Most days, caught in the doing of my work, I didn't remember my morning promise until my drive home. I resolved to try again tomorrow. Occasionally, I remembered when still on the job, but by then, having ridden a wave of anxiety and frustration, my mind refused to be guided to the wonders of me.

I excitedly awaited the dawning of Saturday, and the coming of Joy that it promised. I understood the ideas that arrived in our times together, but now knew I had no clue how to live them in my life. I understood the value of collecting evidence supporting my perfection, but I nevertheless traded it in, day in and day out, for anger, anxiety, and unhappiness. "Why? Why was my misery here at all?" I wondered.

Saturday

February 2

Chapter 17

Rules

I awoke Saturday early in the morning. My body and mind were groggy, both demanding more rest, but my soul, excited by the coming of Joy, refused all attempts at sleep. So I moved slowly out of bed, stumbled into the kitchen and prepared a bowl of cereal.

I moved carelessly through the house, found the bathroom and washed my face, a weak attempt at rejuvenation.

From there I walked down the stairs and out the front door, grabbing the morning paper. I climbed back up, reading the latest misery proclaimed proudly in the front-page headlines.

I moved into the living room, preparing to leaf through the tales of torment that filled my morning paper...

"What the hell?" I shouted as loudly as I could muster at 7:00

a.m. There she was, relaxed and radiant as ever, a vision of love on my living room couch. "Damn it, Joy, you scared the hell out of me."

"I hope so," she said, taking my words literally.

"How did you—?" I stopped the question midway. I wasn't sure I wanted to know how Joy had gotten there; and besides, there were far more important things to talk about. The expression on Joy's face confirmed that

"Hi," I said softly, deciding to start all over again. "It's great to see you."

"As it is wonderful to see you, dearest one. Please, sit, we have much to do on this day."

I sat down, a sense of peace now filling me as I felt the warm embrace of Joy's radiance. Everything seemed perfect when Joy was here. There was nothing I couldn't accomplish, nothing we couldn't do together.

"It is imperative that you understand the value of the lessons learned these past two journeys. Your entire life, and your very experience of it, depends on this."

She had my undivided attention, and she knew it.

"Good," she said, "now let me share a story with you."

Once upon a time, there lived a boy.

This was no ordinary boy. This was a boy who

believed in the vision of his wonder. This was a boy who believed in his perfection. Seeing who he really was, he lived in a way unknown to most today. His rules for life were as simple as they were magnificent, for they were the Rules of the Soul. And his rules were these:

1. Never doubt yourself. You have no reason to because you are perfect just as you are.

2. Whenever there is a decision to be made, simply get in touch with what it is you want, and move yourself freely and easily toward that.

3. Always feel your feelings. If they are happening to you, they are a part of you. You are perfect, so they too must be perfect.

4. Whenever you are faced with adversity, first allow yourself compassion for your hardship. Feel your feelings. Then, simply go for creating what you want in the face of it. Use your adversity as an opportunity to show your passion for love and for life.

5. Delight in everything you see, for just as you are perfect, so too is there perfection in everything around you. See this perfection.

6. Trust and love all that you see. For just as you are worthy of trust and love, so is all else.

7. Give to yourself your very best. Perfection, after all, deserves the best.

One day, this boy lost something of great importance.

This boy lost his vision of perfection. He lost his ability

to see the Divinity of who he was.

Just as a man who loses his vision must rely on other senses to move through the world, this boy, losing his vision of perfection, had to find a new way to move through his life.

Believing now in imperfection, the being invented a new set of rules, rules he created when he looked to the world around him for answers:

1. Doubt yourself. Since there is something down deep that is wrong with you, you cannot trust what it is you know to do.

2. Whenever there is a decision to be made, seek advice. Someone else, someone outside of you, must somehow know better than the imperfect you. Someone else knows what decision is best for you.

3. Be careful what feelings you feel. Feeling happy feelings is okay, as those are pleasing to the people around you. But be careful about those unhappy feelings. People around you don't like those, and there is probably something very wrong with them. Rumor has it that once you start, you may never be able to stop feeling them. Better off keeping those unhappy feelings locked safely inside.

4. Whenever you see yourself acting in a way that is different from what you want—for example, you get frustrated with a friend—judge and condemn yourself...and do it harshly. Tell yourself how terrible and awful you are for doing it, as a way to make sure you never do it again.

5. Be careful not to enjoy the world too much, and

do not be overly grateful for the things you do have. You might get so caught up in enjoying these things and being thankful for them that you'll never do anything to improve yourself further.

6. Do not strive for too much, or you will get hurt. Aim low, that way you won't be overly disappointed.

Although the boy did not like the new rules, he watched everyone around him living by them. He watched a world of beings, perfect at heart, but nonetheless believing in their imperfection, agree without words that these were the rules by which to live. They were never spoken, just understood: a secret code.

"All these giants can't be wrong, and I, a little child, right," the boy told himself. "Since I am imperfect, I shall have to live by these rules too." With a grim resolve, the boy followed these guidelines.

To this day, years later, he still lives by them.

Joy was talking about me, about my life, I was sure of it. "What a sad story, and what a morbid ending," I declared.

"The ending," Joy announced, "has not been written yet. That is up to you."

"You mean I can change it?"

"Of course, dear one, in any moment of your choosing, you are always free to return to the original set of rules.

"However," she warned, "first you must decide that you want

to live by these original rules."

"I do," I declared, remembering how wonderful they sounded. "I really do."

"Yes," she said, "you do in theory. But it is your actions that shout where your words whisper. And I have watched you this week. Your actions betray you."

"You're right," I said, disappointed. I remembered how all week I had rarely been able to collect evidence supporting my perfection. "I tried so hard, Joy. Every morning when I woke up, I told myself, 'Collect the evidence of your wonder, find the moments that prove you're great.' But in no time, the day got the better of me. It was either some nut on the road or the insane rush of my work."

"You say you tried so hard. I say that you do not yet know the meaning of effort. To shift your vision to your wonder, and live by the rules of wonder, you must try as if your life depends on it, because it does."

"But how? How do I make myself remember the new way I want to live? How do I change my way of living for so many years?"

"Two things," Joy said, as I listened with anticipation. "Intention and persistence."

I readied another question, but Joy shook her head as if to say "No," a declaration that now was not the time.

"We have a journey ahead of us, and she is calling us to her now."

Chapter 18

Flight

"Sweet one," Joy began, "do you recall when we went into a state of deep relaxation, how I lead you to the Night of Infinite Possibility?"

"Yes, of course, Joy," I said, wary of where she might be going with her opening.

"Well, that which is possible in the mind's eye is possible in the world," she continued.

I looked her, a puzzled expression coloring my face.

"Everything that fills your house existed first as a thought in someone's mind. It lived there before it took form in your realm of the physical. Your couch," she offered, pointing, "was first a vision before it was born into the physical world. Your TV," she continued, "existed first as a construct in one man's mind before it was turned into the solid reality it is today."

"Okay," I said, agreeing, my tone revealing my curiosity.

"Sweet one, whatever you can imagine, you can create, if only you'd believe. When a great man said, 'You can move mountains if only you have the faith of a mustard seed,' he meant it quite literally. Whatever you imagine, you can create, if first you believe, and then you persist.

"This is a truth of the Universe," Joy continued, "and it holds true for both your internal world and your external world, for both are manifestations of the Divine.

"Now," Joy announced, "in your mind's eye you imagined floating with me, easily and gently in a magnificent night sky. So, if you can float and fly in your mind's eye, then you can …" She paused, waiting for me to finish her sentence.

"…do it for real?" I said, ending her statement with my question.

"Yes," said Joy, visibly amused by the disbelief and excitement expressed in my voice. "Are you ready?"

"I'm going to fly?" my mind asked, still questioning the physical impossibility of this new prospect. "I'm going to fly!" my soul exclaimed, excited that I was finally going to live beyond the limiting confines of my mind.

"Yes, dear one, you are going to fly," Joy responded as she arose, opened the living room window, and offered me her hand.

I put my hand in Joy's, and in that moment of contact, I felt my body rise off the floor, in defiance of the limiting beliefs my physics classes once taught me. "Lucky for me souls don't believe in the limits of physics," I told myself.

I looked over at Joy, who, her hand in mine, hovered with me a foot above the living room floor. I smiled a smile of excitement, delighted by the newfound possibilities of a universe. Joy smiled back, enjoying her vision of my pleasure. We shared a moment of bliss.

She guided me gently, the touch of her hand communicating the fullness of her directions: a quick touch was a stop, a rotation of my hand told me to rotate my body in just the same way. I marveled at how easily, and how much, a simple touch could communicate. For a moment, I wasn't sure if it was the magic of Joy's touch or the act of flight that I enjoyed more.

When Joy flew me out the living room window, I decided it was flying I liked more. We soared out onto Harvard Avenue, floating carefree above the narrow one-way street. Pedestrians and drivers alike seemed to take no notice of us.

"Joy," I asked, "why can't they see us?"

"They do not believe this is possible," Joy replied, "and cannot see that which they do not believe."

Then, as if breaking Joy's rule, a small child on the street corner pointed his finger upward, directly at us, and announced excitedly to the woman by his side, "Mom, look, people, and they're flying!"

Here was someone who had not yet suspended his ability to believe in the magnificent, I thought.

"Now, John," his Mom reprimanded, ready to suffocate his faith, "what did I tell you about lying?"

"But Mommmm..." he began in protest, as we floated upward and out of hearing range.

I looked around as we rose higher into the morning sky, the rush of air blowing my hair into disarray, but invigorating my senses and elevating my excitement. Buildings shrank as we rose, and I could see the city center now, her skyrises shimmering as they touched the morning's light. From up here, everything appeared perfect, as if the universe was unfolding just as it should. "There is a beauty to life that can only be experienced when soaring," I announced.

"This is true, dear one," Joy replied, "but that beauty is seen not only when soaring through air, but also when soaring with spirit."

"Why does everything sound so good when you say it, Joy?" I asked as we flew higher still, now above even the tallest of skyrises in the city center.

"It is not what you say, it is how you say it. The things I say sound good to you because you hear the softness and the love with which I speak, and the tone touches your soul.

"Come," she declared, "it is time we moved on to the Night of Infinite Possibility."

Suddenly we were moving upward at incredible speeds, up first through pillow-like clouds that spotted the morning sky.

"These," she said, wanting to make the most of every opportunity for learning, "are like your fears. The sun of your perfection always shines, but you create clouds of fear that keep you from seeing this sun."

We moved higher still, past a flock of birds in their V-like formation. I tried to think of some wisdom I could glean from the beauty of their flight, hoping to impress Joy with the metaphors I could dream up. But none came into mind.

"Keep practicing," Joy announced, "all things come to those who practice."

"I thought it was all things come to those who wait," I responded, as we flew by a solitary aircraft that dotted the otherwise open sky.

"No," she said, "too many people sit and wait for things to happen in their lives. Too many people are sitting and waiting for their joy to find them. If you want joy, you don't wait, you create. You create by remembering your true nature. But to remember, you must practice, for your illusions are strong in your mind."

We flew higher and higher now, leaving the atmosphere, abandoning the blue color it created for the blackness of space. Soon, we were in the vastness that fills the gaps between stars.

I recognized this place immediately: the Night of Infinite Possibilities.

"Where to tonight?" Joy asked, eager to follow my lead.

I closed my eyes for a moment, taking in a deep breath. On my exhalation, I opened my eyes to the Night. There again, as if by magic, a star called to me. The warmth of her summoning was irresistible, and as I lead Joy by the hand, we floated upward toward my shining star.

She welcomed us with her embrace, spoke kindly to us with her light, and as we moved toward her, her brilliance dwarfed a night sky.

I floated into my star, Joy in hand, ready for another voyage through the doorway of time, ready for whatever adventure my star was willing to offer.

We moved through her tunnel of light, comforted by the gentleness of her soothing embrace. Soon, end in sight, she released us into an old time suddenly new again: 1972.

My eyes adjusted quickly, and I looked around, eager to take in the landscape that surrounded me.

Chapter 19

The Valley of Understanding

A small child played with toy cars at the foot of his bed. The sporty red Camaro in one hand was closely pursued by the police cruiser in the other. Imagined sounds of a high-speed chase escaped the boys mouth. "Mrrrrrr...mm...mm ...mrrrrrrrooommmm!" shouted the boy, mimicking the sounds of a car accelerating as it shifted gears. "Woooow...woooow....woooow," blared make-believe police car sirens in hot pursuit. He was a child lost to the world around him, creating an imaginary universe of delight for his personal pleasure.

The sudden appearance of his parents jolted him back to the reality of the larger world he lived in.

"Hi, sweetie," Mom announced warmly as she walked in the room.

"Hi, son," Dad declared, standing by her side.

He looked up. His concentration broken, he abandoned the high speed chase taking place by his bed.

"Son," Dad continued, "we've got something we'd like to tell you. And it's very exciting news."

The boy looked up tentatively, remembering that what his parents considered exciting was not always that way for him.

"Sweetie," his mom interjected, "we've decided that you don't have enough friends. And, to help you make more friends, we've enrolled you in preschool."

"Preschool," Dad jumped in, the perfection of his timing and the clarity of his words suggesting their practiced nature, "preschool is a place filled with games, and other people like yourself—your size, your age, with your interests. You can go and play with them all day long, and then we'll come and pick you up when the playing is done and you can play some more with us."

"Preschool is a lot of fun," his mom added.

The boy looked up, and from the expression on his face, it was obvious that he was giving careful consideration to his parents' suggestion.

"Well, what do you think? Are you ready to go?"

He continued to think about it for many more moments. Then, with clarity and resolve, more than I remembered ever seeing in a four-year-old, he declared, "No. Thank you. But I'm having fun here. Maybe another time."

Believing this was the end of it, he resumed the high-speed chase he had abandoned just moments earlier.

His parents looked at each other, concern coloring their expressions, sharing an unspoken, "We were hoping it wouldn't come to this."

"Sweetie," his mom said as softly as she could muster, again bringing a quick end to the miniature police pursuit, "your dad and I already enrolled you in the school. We think it's best that you make friends. We want you to go and try it today."

The boy looked up and, with great clarity and disarming honesty, presented a simple solution in line with his wanting. "Please call the school and tell them I'm not coming. I'm happy right where I am.

"Besides," the boy continued, deciding to add evidence to back his declaration, "I have Bucky, my imaginary friend, and he's the best friend in the whole wide world."

His parents looked at each other, concern growing on their faces. This was going to be harder than they had hoped. But it wasn't normal, they had decided, for a boy to spend so much time alone with imaginary friends. Real friends were important in this world, they had told each other, and it was time the boy made some.

"Sweetie," his mom started, speaking gently, but with hints of impatience in her voice, "I'm not sure of the best way to tell you this. But I'm afraid you will be going to that school today. Your dad and I enrolled you, we paid good money to get you in there, and you will go. Today. In fifteen minutes."

The boy didn't know exactly how long fifteen minutes was, but he knew it was soon, a lot sooner than never, which was what he had been lobbying for. His mind left the room for a moment, lost in thought. I wanted to know what he was thinking, so I asked Joy for the glasses. She handed me her rose-colored pair, and as I put them on the world was aglow in rainbows of color. I could see worlds inside and out. I focused on the boy, wanting to learn more of him as the events unfolded.

> I want a way out. I told them I don't want to go, with great clarity, but they aren't willing to listen to what I know to do to take care of myself.
>
> How can I help them understand how much I want to stay home? What can I do to help them see how much my heart and soul wants to be here, not in the preschool of their choosing?
>
> Let me try a big smile and loving words. Why, that helped me get the chocolate chip cookie that I wanted yesterday morning. It could work here too.

"Mom, Dad," the boy said, looking up at his parents. His face softened, and he smiled warmly at them. He even changed the inflection with which he spoke, making his sounds more loving. "I r-e-a-l-l-l-l-y want to be here, and play with my cars and my toys and Bucky. Can you please understand and let me stay here today?"

For a moment, it seemed to him, this just might work. He just might get what it was he wanted: the freedom to stay and play at home. His parents seemed touched by the sincerity and loving nature of the voice.

"Well, Joe," Mom said, "if he really wants to be here, maybe we should trust what it is he wants."

"No, Mary," Dad replied, "we've talked about this, and it's best for him to make friends now. We don't want him alone and isolated his entire life."

His valiant effort had only created one convert, and he would need to convert two if he was going to get what he wanted. His internal world went into overdrive:

What now?

He considered the gamut of emotions he could try on. Joy, laughter, delight, thoughtfulness, calm, serenity. None of these seemed capable of encouraging his parents to listen to the knowing of his heart and soul.

> Wait! Of course. I've seen it on TV and I've tried it a few times in my life. Strangely enough, it seems to work. I don't really know why, but when I do this, Mom and Dad seem to give me all kinds of attention. When I do this, they are ten times more likely to give me what I want. When I do this, more than anything else, my parents understand how much I care about having what I want. Well, I really don't want to go to preschool, and if this is the only way they'll understand how much I want to stay home, then, well, why not?

With that, the boy inhaled deeply, and on the exhalation let out a deep scream. "I don' wanna go!" he bellowed. As if carefully orchestrated by an inner conductor, tears now began to form and flow down his rounded cheeks. Deep sobs followed.

A moment of silence created the brief illusion that the boy was going to stop. That notion was quickly shattered when we all realized that he was just taking in a deep breath to scream and sob all the more loudly on his next exhalation.

As I looked at his parents, I saw the power of the boy's sadness at work. They jumped to action, as if somehow called to arms.

"See, Joe," Mom said, clearly disturbed by her son's tears, "I told you this was a bad idea. I told you he would never go."

This is working, the little boy thought to himself, this is working well. Better make it bigger.

The little actor began to wail now, crying uncontrollably, or so it seemed.

"We've got to do something," Mom declared.

"Listen, he's got to learn to make friends," Dad spoke over the cries of his son.

"Yes, but does he have to do it now?" Mom rebutted. "Should we really be interrupting a world he's so happy in for what we think is right?"

"Of course," Dad responded, "We're his parents, that's why we're here."

But the screams were getting to Dad, too. He was speaking now with less confidence than before. The boy knew he was getting to them. Just a little longer and he would have what he wanted.

Mom walked over and picked him up, attempting to comfort him in her arms. It almost worked. For a moment the tears subsided. But suddenly the little child realized that to forget to cry now would jeopardize everything he had worked so hard for. He was so close to freedom from preschool...he couldn't give in to the comfort of Mom's embrace now. Not yet. With new resolve, the boy returned to his loud cries.

His parents tried a number of different ways to remedy their son's sadness. They brought him water, offered to bribe him with the sweetness of a cookie, told him gently he had to stop this crying, told him loudly he had to stop this crying. But with every failed attempt, they grew in desperation. The boy knew it. He had played out this scene with his parents a few times before. It wouldn't be long now before he had all that he wanted, and could return to the game of cars that had delighted him earlier.

"Okay," Dad finally resolved, "we won't make you go to school today."

Mom smiled at her husband, thanking him for saving their son from his self-inflicted misery.

"Thanks, Mom and Dad," the boy spoke as his sobs subsided. Then, as if nothing had ever happened, the boy returned to his toys, and began his game anew...the miniature police cruiser in a high speed chase with a little red Camaro.

"Joy," I said, the realization of what I had just witnessed starting to sink in, "is this...is this where unhappiness and misery come from?"

Joy waited for me to answer my own question.

"Misery came when I, as a little child, invited it in. I welcomed misery because I understood that she was a powerful motivator in the world around me.

"Smile, be joyous, be a delightful little fellow, and the world is happy to see you, but joy isn't good for getting you what you want.

"Oh, but use misery," I announced, "and the world jumps, quick to try to save you from yourself. A few well-timed tears go a long way in getting you all you want. Some carefully placed anger and the world understands how much you care.

"The squeaky wheel gets the grease, so I squeaked, and I got greased. And I said to myself, 'Look, this squeaking stuff works.' So when I didn't have what I wanted, I squeaked, not because it was a good thing to do or a bad thing to do, but because it worked. I got my grease."

"Yes," Joy said, responding at last, "as a small child, you turned to misery as a helpful tool. You put it on the way you might today put on a T-shirt, a simple tool to help you in your everyday life.

"What you failed to realize," Joy continued, "was that your actions had side effects that even you as a small child could not imagine.

"You got so accustomed to putting on misery, that one day you forgot. You forgot that you were putting on the misery. You began to believe that the misery was an inevitable part of who you are. But you are not misery. You are perfection. You are Divinity. But, alas, you forget."

My mind pieced together Joy's words, and those that danced through me, and at last they spun all that they had heard into a tale too often forgotten:

> Once upon a time, and what a time it was, there lived a newborn being. The being was perfect beyond the boundaries of reason. The being was Divine beyond the realm of understanding. The being trusted himself and all his choices beyond measure.
>
> One day, as the being moved through his life, he was entrusted into the care of giants.
>
> The giants had long since forgotten how to trust themselves, and as a result did not trust much of anyone or anything around them.
>
> The giants certainly did not trust the being, new to their lives, to know what was best for himself.
>
> One day, the giants turned to the young being and told him, "We are sending you away, to a place where you will learn to be just like us."

The being did not want to go, and told them so with the certainty of all that he was. He was clear, confident, and disarmingly honest.

But the giants did not listen to the voice of the being, and told him he would be sent away just the same.

Upon hearing this, the being decided he would try whatever it took to get what he wanted.

The being had seen how, in the past, the giants had responded to great sadness: when someone was sad, they did all they could to save this someone from misery. The being decided it was worth a shot.

The being tried on sadness, wanting to use it as a tool, a tool to tell the giants how much he cared about what he wanted.

The giants responded in predictable fashion, giving in to all the demands of the being. They saved him from his sadness (never realizing the being could save himself from it).

As the being grew in the world, he practiced misery with more and more frequency. Whenever he did not have what he wanted, he turned to misery to help him get that which he wanted.

Unbeknownst to the being, his mind, a tool to help him in life, was watching all this very carefully.

One day, with good intentions, the mind volunteered: "Every time you don't get what you want, I, your mind, will make you sad. That way, you won't have to make any effort at all to create the sadness.

"It will be perfect.

"From now on," the mind continued, "our life will be grand. Either you will have what you want and you will be happy. Or you will not have what you want, and I will tell you to get unhappy so that you will now get what you want, and you can be happy again."

But the being's mind misjudged two things: (1) how often in life the being would not get what he wanted, and (2) the fact that misery would not always work to get the being what he wanted.

Soon, the being, a reflection of the divine, was living not from the divinity within but from a construct of his mind.

His divinity said, "Delight in what you have." But the being listened instead to his mind, which said, "Let's see what you don't have, and get unhappy about that, so that you might get it."

His divinity said, "In the face of adversity, work all the more to create the world you want." But the being listened to his mind, which declared, "In the face of adversity, get unhappy, so that someone will see you in your misery and save you from it."

The truth of the being lay just beneath the surface of misery.

And the truth is this.

Misery is not bad.

Misery is just something the mind learned along the journey of life, as a helpful tool.

Misery lives in life for one reason only: She has been invited in.

We welcomed her as a tool.

Now, she no longer serves us.

We are serving her.

"Now," Joy declared, "you understand how misery has entered into your life. You have seen another truth. In seeing, you begin the act of liberation.

"Come, our time here is up," Joy announced, putting her hand in mine.

As we had before, we again floated heavenward together, hand in hand. Up into the morning sky we flew, and once there, I saw her. She had been waiting for us, refusing to leave with the dawning of day even as her neighboring stars abandoned their twinkling for the light of blue sky. My shining star, our passageway on this journey, summoned us now to travel her warmth back home.

She spoke with her twinkling, invited with the promise of her light, and, as we drew nearer to her, greeted us with the warm glow of her radiance. We entered into her, delighted by the comfort of her embrace. We traveled through the years with her guidance, and as her end neared, she released us into the place I now called home. I felt the gentle rhythms of my body breathing, and the coldness of the floor beneath me, and I knew we had returned.

I awoke my body gently with gradual movement, my eyes the

last to open. There, sitting on the floor beside me was Joy, an abundance of radiance.

"Welcome home," she offered. "There are some learnings that I want to share with you regarding our voyage on this day."

From my lying position, I sat up, my body relaxed from its rest during my spirit's journey. I crossed my legs, and faced Joy. We sat only a foot or two apart. I gave her my undivided attention.

"Good," she said.

"You do a most unusual thing in your life." She paused, as if thinking about the best way to share her insights. "Imagine going to view a movie with someone. When it is all over, you turn to him and tell him how much you loved the movie. He turns to you and tells you how much he disliked it. 'The movie made me cry, it was so powerful and uplifting,' you might say. Meanwhile, your colleague is thinking 'This movie put me to sleep.'

"If a stranger suddenly approached you both, asking each of you 'Why do you feel the way you do now?,' both of you would point to the movie you saw, explaining '*It* is responsible for how I feel.'

"You think it is the movie that made you cry; your friend believes it is the movie that put him to sleep. Other people in the theater decide it was the movie that made them laugh, or that made them sad. Everyone in the theater points an accusatory finger at the movie when it's over, and declares, fingers pointed, 'Look at how I'm feeling now. That movie made me feel this way.' "

"Of course, Joy," I said, wondering what point she could possibly be making.

"But the movie is not responsible for how each person in the theater feels," Joy declared.

I shared my puzzled look with Joy.

"No, dear one, how could one movie make so many people feel so many different ways? The movie is just the external space-time experience. It, like every experience you have, simply invites you to choose how you will respond to it. Do you want to respond feeling your Divinity or do you want to respond feeling your misery? That is your choice. You are not the victim of what the movie does to you, but rather you are free to create your experience, your feelings about the movie as you experience it.

"But people forget. As children, people taught themselves to respond to experience with misery.

"People taught themselves to respond with misery for one reason," Joy said, pausing for dramatic effect. "As a child, misery was a very useful tool.

"But now, people have forgotten that they chose misery long ago. They believe the misery is who they really are. But misery is what hides them from who they really are.

"When people believe in the misery of who they are, they forget their freedom to choose their feelings in each moment. As a result, everyone blames the movie for how they feel. As do you.

"But I tell you this, in the moment you blame the movie for how you feel, you become 'victim.' You become 'disempowered.' You surrender the power that is your birthright. For you cannot change the movie, and you have declared the movie the source of your misery.

"You have the power to change but one thing, and that is the most important of things: yourself. You can learn about yourself, understand why it is you have chosen misery. Then, from that Valley of Understanding, you can create and teach yourself a new way of responding—you can climb the Mountains of Wonder.

"But to liberate yourself from misery and journey to joy, you must first see where you are. You must understand one true thing." Her voice softened, and she spoke in a tone of great gentleness and limitless compassion. "You have chosen misery. You are responsible for any unhappiness you feel. But that, I tell you now, is not incriminating. That is wonderful news. For just as you choose your way in, you can choose your way out. As a small child, you choose misery not to hurt yourself, but to help yourself. As a child of the universe, it is now your right to choose your Divinity, your Joy, your perfection, to help yourself anew."

"But how?" I asked.

"That," offered Joy, "is something so obvious, so apparent, so well-known, that you cannot even see it."

"Joy, help me see it," I said excitedly.

"Next time," she declared. "We have ended our journeys to the Valley of Understanding. You have now heard the three truths of your existence, and they are these. You are Divine. You have forgotten (based on a childhood misunderstanding). Your misery was chosen by you as a child, doing the best you knew in the moment—just as you chose misery then, you can choose joy now."

With that she arose and let herself out. Our Saturday journey had come to an end.

Saturday

February 9

Chapter 20

Building Castles of Joy One Brick at a Time

With each new Saturday came the dawning of new hope and the renewed promise of journeys with Joy. This Saturday was no exception, and my excited soul woke my weary body from bed well before he was ready. "No matter," my mind spoke, "there is time enough for rest on Sunday. Today let's greet the coming of Joy."

I was noticing something strange going on in my mind this morning. She seemed far less fearful and increasingly excited about the coming of Joy.

"It is because mind is no longer threatened," a thought popped in.

"Yes, mind thought you were going to follow soul to the point where you would lose your mind," its neighbor continued.

"But mind no longer has that fear. She knows now that soul sees the value of mind; a useful tool in understanding the world around you," another thought spoke.

"Soul wants to change your mind so you can change your life, not lose your mind. Soul wants to change your mind so that it is a vehicle of your spirit. Soul wants to change your mind so it helps you carry out your spirit work," another thought declared.

"And that's okay with mind. She's tired of working against the soul," my thoughts all declared in unison.

"What?" I asked, unable to piece together the thinking of my mind. Thoughts responded with a short story, knowing I understood best that way.

> Once upon a time, there lived beings made up of body and soul, but no mind.
>
> Each being moved her body through the world in perfect harmony with all that was around her, living through the instinct of the soul.
>
> One day, there was a most miraculous birth. Born that day was a being with something new, something called mind. She, then, had body, mind and soul.
>
> Her mind was a gift from the Divine, providing her a second outlet for the expression of who she was— with body she could create through action, as those around her did. With mind, she could create through thought and word, a new expression of her soul.

But a very strange thing happened along the way. The being began to live in her mind, letting her mind guide her life, not her soul. As she did this, she lost sight of who she really was, for it was her soul that communicated this message.

The being began to wander through her life, wondering what her purpose was, trying to get her mind to answer what only her soul could speak.

The mind was a gift to help the soul express itself more fully, and could serve no purpose but this. Her mind could not tell the being why she was here or what she was to do.

Then one day a second being came, and offered her the opportunity to get out of her mind. The new being promised a return to living through soul. At first the mind rebelled, fearful of losing control. But, as the soul began to speak, all understood, even the mind, that life was meant to be guided by the soul.

I understood now what my mind was telling me, and why she was growing in excitement at the coming of Joy.

I moved through the house, lost in the thoughts of my story, paying no particular attention to the world around me.

"What the...?" I shouted, jolted back into my surroundings by the sudden presence of Joy, aglow on my living room couch. My soul leaped with delight as I saw her, and a broad smile quickly painted my face the expressions of happiness. It was Joy! She was here again!

"I am so glad you are here," I announced. "It is such a delight to see you."

"As I am always delighted to see you, sweet man," she replied. "We have much to learn this Saturday; are you ready for our journey?"

"Joy," I declared, "I've been ready my whole life!"

"Yes, indeed," she said, "you have. And now, at last, you realize it."

"So where to?" I asked, expecting and excited about a return to the Night of Infinite Possibilities.

"First, we will voyage with words," she offered softly in reply.

"With words? Where can you go with words?" I asked. My disappointment that we were not heading off on a journey to a different space and time colored my tone.

"Why, my dear friend," Joy offered, the softness of her voice my consolation, "with words you can travel here, there and everywhere."

"So what are we talking about?" I asked as I seated myself comfortably on the plush living room chair, readying myself for this new way of adventuring.

"What would you like to talk of?" she offered softly in reply, answering my question with hers.

Suddenly, thoughts unanswered from our time together last Saturday jumped to mind.

"*How* do you do it?" I asked.

"*How?*" I continued. "I understand the visions I saw of myself as a child. I chose unhappiness then. I surrendered my belief in my wonder then.

"So, *how*, now, all these years later, do I undo it? How do I change my mind, so it now chooses joy? How do I believe again in my wonder and Divinity?

"I understand where I am, why I'm here and where I want to be," I continued before Joy could answer. "I see I'm living misery because I chose misery a long time ago, and I doubt my value because I gave up believing in me a long time back. I also know now where I want to be. I want my mind to choose happiness, and I want my mind to believe in my wonder.

"But what I don't get are the steps in between. How do I go from the misery I am to the wonder I want to be?"

"Silly, silly, sweet man," Joy replied, "you know exactly how, but you refuse to see. You imagine there to be some magic trick for getting from here to there. But there is no magic trick. The way from here to there is, as it has always been for you, the very same journey.

"You hope," Joy announced, "that I will tell you some mystical way to get to the happiness you want. You hope that I will give you some ruby slippers. You will put these on, tap them three times and say, 'I want to go home,' and then home, your home of happiness and joy everlasting, you shall be. Is that not correct?"

I nodded my head in agreement. I would have loved some ruby slippers.

"And yet, down deep, a part of you knows there is no such way. And 'thank God' that part of you says. For where would your personal power be if I gave to you your happiness?

"You desperately want the opportunity to stand up and create the life you dream possible, and if I gave it to you now on a silver platter, you would be denied the delight of creating it.

"You are a creator," Joy continued, "and the way to make what you want in your life is to create it; to build it one step at a time. When people want to construct a brick home, first they lay a foundation, and then they lay one brick on top of another. In time, they have completed their home. They do not close their eyes, wish for the house to be built, then open their eyes and hope it is there. You understand this principle with house building. Yet you have been refusing to believe it when it comes to your own joy."

I was starting to catch on. In my enthusiasm, I jumped in. "Like when I decided I wanted to get a college degree. Once I decided I wanted one, I didn't go to bed at night, pray to God that he would give me the degree, and hope the next morning one would be there, hanging on my wall," I shared, amused by the imagery my words had created.

"I decided if I wanted a college degree, then I'd have to make that happen. So I registered at the university and took classes. The first semester was really tough. I didn't know exactly what my professors expected or how to deal with all the work that was assigned to me. But I stuck with it. I wanted that degree so much that there were times I worked sixteen-hour days to make it happen. I never gave up. It took four years, but in the end, I emerged degree in hand, having created what I wanted in my life."

"Yes!" Joy declared, my enthusiasm becoming her excitement. "As with everything, the journey to creating a life of happiness..."

"You take it one step at a time. You decide you want it, and you work to make it happen." I was getting the hang of this idea. "You live it one day at a time, and over the weeks and months, you build your happiness-making skills. Choosing happiness becomes easier and easier, and in four years you go to the hardware store, buy a blank certificate, fill it in with your name, and give yourself an honorary degree in the school of joy."

"Yes," said Joy, "you have just made your first realization in the *how* of living joy."

"There is more to it than that?" I asked, believing I had now understood it all.

"There are gems of wisdom that can help you on this journey to creating joy one moment at a time. There are things to know and to do that will help make this act of creation a reality. When, in school, you took a physics class," Joy continued, "the math skills you had learned helped you in that class. In much the same way, to learn to live Joy, there are a multitude of tools that will help facilitate your journey."

"And you're going to teach me those?"

"Yes," Joy said, "and that is all I can do. I have given you the awareness of where you are, that you could begin this journey from the Valley of Understanding. For all true journeys begin here.

"Now I will give you the Tools of Happiness, that you might use them to climb the Mountain of Wonder. But I cannot climb that mountain for you. As we have spoken, that is a voyage only you can take. For it is you who decides where you go, when, and how quickly.

"However," Joy declared, "somewhere along the journey to the heights of joy, all true travelers discover one true thing. Each traveler realizes that they are and have always been one with the entire Mountain of Wonder. In that moment of all-encompassing realization, they liberate themselves to decide where they want to be in any moment of their journey, and in the next moment they are there."

I gave Joy what was, by now, a familiar puzzled expression.

"You shall understand that which I just said when you are ready," was all she offered in reply.

Chapter 21

The Invention of Intention

"Come," Joy announced, "we have shared enough with words for now."

With that declaration, Joy put out her hand, offering me its gentle embrace. I accepted, placing my hand in hers. In the moments following contact, I felt myself once again lift off from the living room floor. An inch above the reassurance of wood planks, I hovered, Joy by my side, delighted by the freedom of flight.

We glided through the living room and to the window. Opening it with little effort, we glided out, and for a second time flew out over Harvard Avenue. Thirty feet above ground, I experienced the wondrous freedom of flight, gliding freely through the three dimensions of space.

Our path took us out past nearby railroad tracks, memories of the city's past, now converted to accommodate the multitude of bicyclists who today filled her cement paths. We continued our journey, floating over car-filled and people-crowded Sherbrooke Avenue. People hurried through the streets, as if each was on a personal mission to save the world. We left the hustle of sidewalk streets for a traffic-jammed Decarie Freeway, where cars moved more slowly than people. There they sat, motionless, bumper-to-bumper, a blending of size, shape and color. The visions of high speeds that drivers had optimistically imagined were now a distant memory.

We started a descent toward the stream of traffic, readying to enter into it. Then, suddenly, below us, I recognized an ocean-blue Toyota Tercel, its rusted side and hatchback rear marking it clearly as my own.

"Joy," I shouted, "someone's stolen my car. We've got to go down there and get it back."

She looked at me amused, as if once again I had completely misunderstood the possibilities she was presenting.

She said nothing in response, continuing instead to lower us on our journey into the heart of freeway traffic. It was when I realized she was directing us toward my car that I silenced my protest.

We floated down through the noises of traffic: cars honking; engines revving; trucks shifting into gear, followed by sounds of acceleration and squeaking breaks; a motorcycle impatiently navigating its way between cars in narrow lanes of traffic. The sights and sounds of it brought a familiar tension to my shoulders. Joy, on the other hand, appeared as calm and confident as ever, a radiant glow in a sea of morning madness. "She's probably never driven through it," I thought to myself.

We entered my blue Toyota Tercel through an open window, and together we squeezed into the passenger seat. I readied myself to take a good look at the driver, wanting reassurance that I could identify him in the police lineup once Joy and I turned him in. But when my eyes caught sight of the driver, I realized there would be no point studying his features. They were all undeniably recognizable.

"Joy," I said, startled, "how can that be me driving the car? I'm right here, with you."

She smiled, her usual response to my disbelief. "Well, sweet man, when we traveled through the dimensions of space, we also floated ever so slightly through the doorways of time."

"Where...no...when are we?"

"This is your future. It is Monday morning, and this, as you likely recognize, is your drive to work."

"Why are we here?" I said, displeased with where this voyage had taken us. I would be experiencing the distress of the traffic soon enough.

"All things in the fullness of time. For now, watch, listen and hold on to your socks. You're in for the ride of your life."

Joy handed me her pair of rose-colored glasses, and motioned for me to put them on. In moments, the world around me was aglow once again with color, and internal worlds of thought were transparent to me. I listened to the rhythms of my Monday morning mind.

> Remember what Joy said. Intention. Intention. Intention. Intention is the first Tool of Happiness you're going to use to climb the Mountain of Wonder. What was it she had said? Oh, yes, that it's a lot easier to climb a Mountain if you remember why you are on the Mountainside in the first place.

> Remember, my intention today is to be joyful. Be joyful. That's what I ultimately want in my life.

The signal light on the car to our immediate left winked at us, indicating the driver's intention to turn into our lane. He began his slow turn in heavy traffic, readying to squeeze himself into the small space between our car and the white Ford Taurus in front of us. The colors around the Monday-morning Me suddenly changed, bright lights dimming.

> You scoundrel. Cutting in front like that is dangerous. You'll get us both killed with those moves.

Thoughts of anger filled my Monday-morning mind, suffocating all thinking from earlier times. The car in the left lane completed his squeeze into the small space in front of us. We had to brake hard to avoid hitting him, even at the slow speeds of rush-hour traffic. The Monday-morning Me shared my displeasure over the dangerous maneuver through loud honks and shouts of discontent.

"Look deeper," Joy announced.

"What do you mean?"

"Use the rose-colored glasses. With them, you can see beyond the anger, to the thinking and the intention beneath the feeling.

"Don't ask me how," she stated, preempting my next question. "Just decide you want to see more, and the glasses will do the rest."

Trusting Joy beyond doubt, I used her words as my internal guide, and made an unspoken declaration that I wanted to see deeper. As soon as I decided, it seemed to me, the glasses acquiesced.

> I really didn't want to get angry, but that scoundrel with his lousy driving gave me no choice. It's his fault I feel this way. He nearly forced me into an accident, and his terrible driving made me angry.

I watched as the Monday-morning Me acted in ways Joy had prophesized. I was blaming the outside world, the "movie" that was unfolding before me, for how I felt. I could see, in that moment, how I believed myself a victim of an external world of insane drivers.

"Deeper," I heard myself tell the glasses, as if a part of me knew that there was far more to this event than I had yet seen and heard.

> I want the driver to know that it is not OK with me that he cut in front of me like that. It is not what I

want him to do. Ever. And I need some way to communicate that to him.

How do you tell people you don't want them to do things?

You get angry with them, of course. That way, they see how much you want something different, and they see that what they are doing is wrong.

If I don't get angry at that driver, he'll never stop acting in this way. If I don't get angry at the driver, he'll never know I want him to do something different.

"Joy, did I hear that right?"

She looked at me, her eyes inviting me to continue before she spoke.

"It sounded to me like just beneath the surface of my anger, and my willingness to blame the other driver for how I felt, was a very profound awareness.

"It sounded like I knew that I was choosing to get angry. I was choosing to get angry because I believed my anger would serve a useful purpose. Anger would be the best way I knew to tell the driver to stop doing the things I don't want."

"Yes, sweet one," Joy said, breaking her silence with the softness of her voice, "you have indeed *chosen* to get angry for just this reason."

"Joy, do you know what this means?" I declared, asking a question I had every intention of answering for myself. "This means I *chose* to get angry because I thought the driver would learn a lesson from my anger.

"Joy, if I chose to get angry to get what I want, maybe I can find a different way to get what I want, without the anger. Then, I could drive through rush hours without the frustration.

"But how? I see the possibility, but I don't see how to live it?"

"The first step to creating joy," she offered in reply, "is remembering your freedom. And remembering that joy is what you want to do with that freedom. That is *intention*.

"Intention is the first Tool of Happiness used in any climb up the Mountain of Wonder. It is far easier to climb a Mountain if you remember why you are standing on the Mountainside in the first place. Remember that your intention is always, first and foremost, to be joyful.

"Then," Joy continued, "with that simple beginning, the story will look like this on Monday morning."

A bright flash of light lit the world in bright yellows and whites, and when vision returned, there we were again, sitting by a Monday-morning Me, a minute into the past. A white Ford Taurus crawled ahead in front of us, the car to the left had yet to make her anger-inducing turn into our lane.

I watched the Monday-morning Me, this time colored in brighter lights, lost in thought, sharing inwardly the importance of intention. My thoughts were interrupted, in the exact same manner as before, by the car in the left lane signaling her desire to enter the small space in front of us. Her metallic body moved, following the lead of her signal light, and there was no doubt of her intention. She would move into this lane, forcing us to brake hard or hit her.

Feelings of anger began to bubble up from the insides of the new Monday-morning me. But this time, something most unusual happened. I listened to the thoughts in a new mind:

> Slow it down. Slow down your car and slow down your mind. Remember your intention. Remember your intention. Remember what you saw with Joy.

He was making a valiant effort, but the seeds of anger were breaking through the soil of his intentions.

> I want to get angry at this driver to teach him a lesson in driving.

Suddenly, the wisdom of his soul broke through, presenting the Monday-morning Me with two questions as simple as they were wise.

> Is my well-being worth giving up over this?

> Do I really want to abandon my intention for a joyous life so I can teach some stranger a lesson?

The questions jolted him back to his original intention.

> No! Joy is my new priority.

He grew in his determination to maintain his joy.

As I looked again, I saw the beginnings of profound transformation. He was not only going to maintain joy, remembering his intention, he was going to do far more than that.

> I not only want to maintain my emotional well-being, I also want to tell this driver that I don't want him to drive this way.
>
> I'll have to find a way without anger to communicate to him what I want. So, how do I tell this driver I don't want him to cut in front of me, or anyone else, without getting myself angry?

Wow, I thought, in this future, I was going to have it all—my joy and the sharing of my message.

> Well, what if I tried getting just a little angry at him? Will that teach him a lesson, telling him how much I don't want him to do this again?
>
> A little anger would be better than a lot.
>
> Thinking about that now, from a calmer place, will my anger really teach the other driver anything? When I honk and yell at him, he'll probably think I'm some jerk, and he'll honk and yell back. My anger, which I thought was telling him to never do what he just did again, would really just create two angry people.

That future me is right! I thought. All this time, driving through traffic, I've been getting angry at drivers, honking and yelling when they do crazy things like cut in front of me. I was always believing I was teaching them a lesson through my anger, but maybe all I was doing was creating two angry drivers.

You know, as I think about this, there really isn't anything I can communicate to this driver, with me in my car and he in his, that would tell him in a way he could hear, "I want you to drive differently."

Since I can't communicate what I want, I'll just let it go.

I'll trust that the universe will take care of this in its own time. If he continues to drive like that, he ends up creating an accident, and that may be the only way he learns.

As simply as that, the future me just let it go. There was no condemnation, no anger, no honks and no angry words. In its place, a peaceful, playful energy filled the car on that morning drive to work, as similar scenes played themselves out in rush hours of traffic.

"Joy," I began, turning to her in the cramped space of the passenger seat, "we just saw two possible futures, didn't we?"

She nodded her head in affirmation.

"Which one will happen?" I asked.

"The two you have seen are but two in an ocean of infinite possibilities," she replied. "That which you will experience is entirely up to you."

With those words, she offered me her hand. I accepted, delighting in the softness of her touch. Together, we floated heavenward once again, above the sights and sounds of traffic. We reversed our earlier path and soon returned to the comfort of my living room. As we landed gently on the wood-covered floor, I turned to Joy by my side, seeking deeper understandings.

"Joy, was the only difference between the two me's we saw intention?"

"Intention is always the beginning of the difference. Without it, none of what you saw would have been there for the seeing. All greatness begins with great intention.

"Anytime you are feeling angry or sad," Joy continued, "it is because you are believing in the power of anger and sadness in your life. You are believing it can help you create that which you want.

"Together, we journeyed and saw how as a child you turned to sadness to tell parents how much you cared about staying home from preschool. Today, you saw how you turned to anger to tell a driver how much you wanted him to stop acting in ways you did not like.

"The value of anger and sadness has been taught to you, by you, time and time again. It now helps you get the things you want in life. Or so you believe.

"What you must always ask yourself is this: What is it you want most of all? When you look back on your life, what do you most want to see?

"At last, you have realized that most of all you want your joy and your laughter. You have realized that as you lie on your deathbed you want to see and remember a life of times fully lived with joy.

"Now, to do that, you must first remember. You must remember in every moment of your life what you want most of all. For this memory will shape the decisions you make in the next moment, and these decisions will shape you."

She paused, as if deciding whether or not she was done.

"In life, you will see two types of moments," Joy declared, continuing. "There will be moments in which, through external experience, you get what you want, and there will be moments in which you don't.

"In moments that you get what you want externally, you will know joy internally, for that is one way to journey to joy.

"In moments that you do not get what you want externally, you must first remember that which you most want internally in this life, above all else: your joy. To remember, ask yourself, always, in those moments, 'Is my internal well-being worth sacrificing over this external factor?' Remembering your intention is joy, always answer with a resounding, 'No!' With no, your joy is no longer in jeopardy."

A story came to and through me then, with words inspired by Joy's:

> Once there lived a creature. Forgetting the perfection that she was, she believed in the misery that she was not.

She lived a life of quiet desperation.

Each day was spent drowning in pools of anger and tides of frustration.

Whenever her world did not give her that which she wanted, she turned to the heavens, and shouted

a pained "Why me?",

an enraged "How could you do this to me?" or

a sad "Why are you punishing me in this way?"

At home alone at night, the being would cry tears of agony, wishing and praying for an end to her days of misery.

But these were the only moments that she remembered her desire for peace.

For every morning, like the one before, as the perceived injustices of her world surrounded her, she would abandon her thoughts of peace. In its place, she screamed once more to the Gods in the heavens, bemoaning her fate.

Then one day, with the inspiration of her soul, she realized but one thing.

"If I would be joyous, I could start from within, and work my way out. I could create from the inside out the change I always dreamed possible, rather than waiting for it to go from the outside in."

And so into this being was born that day the Invention of Intention.

She declared to herself and the world around her:

"I am joy. I am living joy, and joy shall be all I know. No one and no thing shall ever derail me from my newfound experience of life. Each moment shall I remember that which I want and that which I am defining myself to be, and in each moment, that shall I be!"

Suddenly, as if her declaration held the power of a Force of Nature, shift happened.

When adversity came her way, she declared, "I am living joy, and nothing shall derail me from that which I am." With this memory of the Invention of Intention, she began her journey to internal well-being even in the face of her external adversity.

Chapter 22

Judgment and the Reality of Duality

J oy looked at me, deciding if we were done for the day.

"Joy," I said, reading her expression, then sharing my wanting, "I'm just getting started. I see intention as the first step to joy. It's clear to me that there's no way I can find joy if I forget I want it."

"But," I continued, presenting a case for her continued sharing, "even remembering I want happiness, I'm not sure how to create it when things don't go my way."

Joy paused, as if deciding the best way to begin. "The ability to respond simply with joy was lost to you the very moment you lost sight of the perfection that you are. It is this lost vision that causes you to forget to live the ease of joy.

"The fastest way to reclaim your joy, and your ability to choose it in every and any moment, is belief. Believe in your wonder.

"And I would tell you this: believe in the perfection of you, and you shall never know another moment of unhappiness.

"But this is too much for you. For your distrust of yourself is great. And to ask this of you now is too big and daunting a task."

She was right. I had no idea how to simply believe in my wonder. Most of the time I saw myself as an unhappy person struggling to make it through each day with some semblance of personal well-being left when it was done. I certainly didn't feel perfect.

"A mother blends food before giving it to a small child, so the child might eat without choking while benefiting from its nutrients," Joy continued, her voice soft and her rhythm calming. "So too shall we, on this day, blend our understanding of your perfection into smaller, more manageable pieces.

"In time, just as a small child grows teeth and can soon eat the whole without the blending, so too will your practice with the pieces of perfection help you grow internally, until, at last, you are ready to believe again in your wonder. In the moment that you do, you will know joy beyond measure."

It sounded like a great plan to me. Give me my wonder, one piece at a time, in ways I could live it, until I got the hang of this joy practice. Then maybe I'd be ready for something bigger.

"There are many levels on which your lost belief in your wonder takes you down a path of misery, blinding you to your birthright of joy. And there are simple ways in which to bring you back."

The rhythms with which she spoke were captivating, the choice of her words prophet-like, and I imagined myself first in some great Buddhist temple hearing the words of the Dalai Lama, then in some ancient Middle Eastern landscape, listening to Jesus deliver the sermon on the mount. Joy had a way with words.

"We shall engage first in words, in talk," she said, as if seeing my great delight in her spoken word, "that you might begin with understanding. Then, we shall travel the road of your experience, that you might *know* that which you will understand."

Joy had my undivided attention. I looked at her, her eyes aglow with her radiance, emanating a mesmerizing blend of gentleness and confidence as she spoke. She appeared in that moment the daughter of Compassion and Empowerment. She began to spin a story as captivating as it was mysterious.

> Once upon a time, and what a time it was, there lived a world inhabited by beings beautiful beyond even their wildest imaginings.
>
> On this world, life defined itself in pairs, and there existed the Reality of Duality.
>
> First was the Duality of Experience. Here, in each external experience, a being either received that which she wanted, or she received that which she did not want.

Second, was the Duality of Response. In response to any external experience, the being could respond in one of two ways. She was free to respond with Love, living from the perfection of that which she was. She was also free to respond with fear, living life from that which she was not.

Each being, aware of her perfection, saw the Duality of Experience and declared:

"As we are Reflections of Perfection, so too must all that surrounds us be Reflections of Perfection. Each experience granted us by the universe, through the Duality of Experience, can only be perfect.

"Let us take every perfect experience, and know each as an opportunity to better live the Love that we are."

In getting that which she wanted, each being responded with celebration and delight in the abundance of the universe.

In getting that which she did not want, each being transformed the experience into opportunity. She created a passion to go for that which she wanted all the more, with added conviction and daring.

Theirs was a life of unbounded joy and wonder, for what else could beings that believed this was their birthright experience? It was celebration when getting what they wanted, and passion, daring and conviction when they did not. Life was naught but unbounded delight.

እ፦   እ፦   እ፦

Somewhere along their journey through life, the beings lost sight of their perfection. In so doing, so too did they lose sight of their perfect way of living.

The beings searched for a new way of living, a way that worked for them when they misplaced the Truth that they were.

Searching, they found a tool to move them through a life suddenly wrought with imperfection.

The tool was called Judgment.

With this discovery, life would never know the state of wonder that she once was, and was always meant to be.

For Judgment transformed the Reality of Duality.

First, Judgment turned the Duality of Experience into the Battle of Good and Bad. With Judgment, the experience of getting what the being wanted was called "good." With Judgment, the experience of not getting what the being wanted was called "bad." Of course, good and bad were not truth, but rather illusions Judgment placed on truth.

Next, Judgment turned the Duality of Response into the Struggle of Good and Evil. Whenever a being responded with love, Judgment called this "good." Whenever a being responded with fear, Judgment called this "evil." While the freedom to choose between love and fear was the truth of existence, Judgment named these Good and Evil.

Judgment, once in the beings' lives, insisted that the Battle of Good and Bad, and the Struggle of Good and Evil, were reality and not illusion.

Soon, seeing with the eyes of Judgment, each being found a new way of living, a way that took her away from the Land of Perfection, and away from the Plains of Joy.

"In the face of adversity," Judgment declared to each being, "start with the word Bad, calling the adversity terrible and awful. Turn your cries into feelings of sadness, anger, and ultimately rage. That will motivate the world to change."

๛　๛　๛

While each being used Judgment to motivate change, the change most dearly wanted was a return to the Plains of Joy.

Each soul knew the Way to Joy, but the Way scared the hell out of the beings:

"Let go of calling the world good and bad, and people good and evil. Instead trust in the perfection of that which you are, and the perfection that the world around you offers. In so doing, you will return to the divine truths of the universe, and there you will see beyond the illusions of judgment, and view the wonder that is you."

๛　๛　๛

One day a being appeared who listened to the calling of his soul and heard the truth of life. He told the world all that which he heard. And for this, he was called a prophet.

The prophet began to speak of the illusions of the world, declaring that there was no such thing as the Battle of Good and Bad, nor the Struggle of Good and Evil, but rather there could be but the Duality of Experience, and the Duality of Response.

As one heard him speak, and the words moved into his heart, he turned and spoke to the prophet, voicing his mind's final protest, "Oh, come on, everyone else knows that there is good and evil."

"You were not put here to live what everyone else knows," the prophet offered gently, "but rather to live that which you know. And the knowing of your soul surely tells you that which I speak is Truth.

"I tell you now, with as much assurance as I have ever spoken before: if you seek happiness and joy, then you must be willing to surrender the illusions of the mind and replace them with the Divine Knowing of the soul."

As the prophet spoke, and many came to listen, he took the ways of old and made them new again. He taught them how to live with Joy, and his tool for a life beyond Judgment was as simple as it was true.

"First, whenever you are faced with adversity, be aware of the two choices before you. It is the Duality of Response. One choice is founded in love, the other is grounded in fear. To help yourself remember which choice to make, always ask but this of yourself:

'What part of me do I wish to experience now?' or

'Is my well-being really worth giving up over this?'

"Remembering, which is the Invention of Intention, that your top priority in life is your joy, then always decide that you want to experience your love, and that your well-being is not worth giving up, not ever.

"With that decision in hand, now tell yourself but this:

'Let me know compassion for myself in the face of adversity; let me remember that it is in times of hardship that I most need my own support and understanding.'

"Breathe deeply, and feel but compassion for all where you are.

"In the space of compassion, allow yourself all the feelings that may arise. Feel everything that comes to you, allowing it to move freely through you. Comfort yourself as if you were your only child.

"This may look at one time like treating yourself to chocolate ice cream, and another time like allowing the sadness within to bubble forth in tears. Remember always that to feel your feelings is to move through them.

"In this way, you will allow the part of you that does not believe in your wonder to be felt, heard, and released, and it shall not stand in the way of your most wondrous next step.

"Now, whenever you are ready, ask yourself:

'What do I seek to create for myself in the face of the adversity?'

"Work next only to create that. The energy once spent judging and condemning the world, take this very energy and invest in the bank of your creation, that you might manifest that which your heart and soul desires.

"Understand now how to live the truth beyond the illusion of good and bad, beyond the construct of good and evil. Let there be only what is. And turn what is into an expression of love."

And with that the prophet walked away. And each in the land decided where it was they would journey from there.

"Joy," I declared, returning to my reality when her tale was done, "are you suggesting there's no such thing as good and bad?"

"I am suggesting that there is far more in your world than you can see through the limited vision of your judgments.

"Come," she offered, holding out her hand, "and you can see for yourself."

Chapter 23

Beyond the Illusion of Judgment

I took her hand, expecting that together we would float upward into the vastness of sky. Instead, Joy gently lay me down on the coldness of the living room floor, and placed herself comfortably by my side. I closed my eyes, anticipating what was to come. With the wisdom of her words, Joy guided me on a journey to a place of deep calm, deep inside.

It started with her invitation to focus on my breath.

"Allow yourself," Joy spoke, softly and with great warmth, "to take three deep breaths. Inhale deeply...Let go. Breath deep...Release. Inhale deeply...let go. In that final release, feel your breath return to its own natural rhythms."

Joy welcomed me next to the fullest experience of my breath.

"Feel the filling of your lungs as they take in the essence of life, and their liberation as they free themselves in preparation for their next inhalation. Filling...liberating. Life...freedom. Essence...room for essence."

Her words were an experience in divinity.

"Add now the experiences of the movement of life. Feel the air's flow as it moves through your nostrils and down your windpipe, and then its return, transformed, as it moves its way back from rising and falling lungs, returning to the place whence it came. The flow of air in...the dance of the lungs...the freedom of release. The flow in...the dance of the lungs...air's gentle release.

"And now, adding to the symphony of your experience, feel also the rise and fall of your stomach, as it too, participates in the Perfection of Life that is the breath. And so it goes," she continued, leading me through the fullness of my inner experience, "the flow and movement of life into you...the lungs filling and the stomach rising in greeting...their release and gentle falling in liberation...and the flow of air out from whence it came."

I was lost to the outside world, lost to the inner world of my breath, its movements a calming presence like none I had ever felt before.

"There is nowhere to go," Joy began, as if inviting me to maintain this wondrous experience for all time. "There is nothing to do," Joy continued, as I remained in the fullness of my breath.

"There never has been, and there never will be," she continued, using words my mind did not understand, speaking with words that calmed my soul. The more she spoke, the more deeply I felt my body relax.

"Just be here and now," Joy spoke, "for that is all there ever is, and all there ever shall be." The rhythm of my breath and the song that was Joy's words together had me aglow in the delight of life.

"Allow yourself," Joy continued, her words an open invitation that I would now never refuse, "to begin a journey into the depth of your perfection."

As Joy spoke, she slowed her pace to a near stop, enunciating every word as if it were the most important ever spoken. "Feel deep within you a place. It is no ordinary space, but rather it is a place of unreasonable compassion and unconditional love. Feel the welcome of this space deep within.

"Wanting to freely fall into its wonder, allow yourself to float gently downward toward this space. Feel yourself, in no particular hurry, floating easily and freely toward this inner paradise. Deeper and deeper," Joy continued, her words almost hypnotic, "deeper...and ever deeper."

I was adrift in an internal world, guided to the chasms within by the rhythms of a breath suddenly alive through awareness, and by the soft callings of Joy's words. I could see in me, deep within, a space radiating, much as Joy always did, the light of compassion and divinity. This space called to me, and, drifting deeper and deeper, I followed its summons.

"Allow yourself," Joy continued, "to enter into the space of unreasonable compassion and unconditional love that lives deep within you. Feel yourself, at last, returning home, the place you have so desperately sought outside of you, now alive within.

"As you enter the radiance of this space," Joy spoke, comfort and confidence both alive in her voice, "feel a warmth on your back, as if the sun's shine is caressing it gently.

"Adrift in the wonder of your space, look down," Joy guided, "and in your mind's eye, envision yourself floating, floating over a wondrous deep blue ocean, its seas calmed by the softness of the sunlit day."

In the moment she spoke it, I could see it. There I was, gliding effortlessly through air as if a seagull, warmed by the sun's embrace, delighting in a spacious deep blue sea that covered the landscape beneath me.

"Joy!" I exclaimed, seeing her in the distance, floating gently toward me. As much as I delighted in the wonder of this space, it seemed somehow twice as nice with Joy by my side.

She floated her way to my side. Together, in silence, we shared the harmony of this deep inner experience. The ocean sparkled beneath us, aglow with gems, each a sparkle of sun reflecting off her surface. The wind was both gentle and warm, and her currents carried us over the sea that stretched to the ends of forever. These were moments of perfection uninterrupted.

My mind noted something in the distance, a break in the water. I squinted, a weak attempt to view it more clearly, but it was lost in the horizon.

Whatever it was, we were floating gently toward it.

As we drew nearer, I could see it now all the more clearly. Land, a small piece of it, standing out boldly, surrounded on all sides by the vastness of ocean.

Yet this was no ordinary island. Even from this distance I could see the almost magical quality surrounding her. She was calling to me, beckoning me to come and discover the delight of her shores.

"This," Joy declared, "is your very own Island of Paradise. It has lived within you all these years, waiting patiently for the time when you would be ready to journey to her. She watched as you searched for her in the world around you, knowing that when you were ready, you would find yourself at her shores deep inside. Here she has sat, from the beginning of your time, wanting only to embrace you with her welcome, and share with you her wisdom."

"I'm so glad that I've found her," I said, delighted by all that was around me then.

"As she is so glad that at last you have found her," Joy replied, the voice of my Island of Paradise.

We floated gracefully toward her shores. She offered us her beach of soft sand for our landing. We accepted her invitation, and hand in hand, landed safely on her shores.

"Take moments and fully experience this place," Joy offered, "it has taken you a long time to arrive. There is no hurry. Delight in what you are at last ready to behold."

I let the warm sand cascade through my toes and tickle the bottoms of my feet. I headed for the sea, wading in her calm clear waters, feeling the ripples of the waves and the gentle pull of her mild undertow. I lost track of time as I danced in those shores of magnificence.

Soon, the sky above began the changing of her colors. The sun, showering us so generously with her warmth just moments before, was preparing to take leave. Her counterpart was already awake in a soon-to-be night sky.

I sat on the shore, delighted by the changing sky, as she transformed blues to yellows, yellows to oranges, and finally oranges to reds. The sun, having said her goodnight, moved gently into the horizon, disappeared and gave way to the beauty of a starlit night sky. Looking up, I recognized the vision at once. This was the Night of Infinite Possibility, and here I sat, on my Island of Paradise, enchanted by her presence.

With the departure of the sun's embrace, I felt a sudden chill. I turned, preparing to talk with Joy. But, much to my surprise, she was nowhere to be found. I began to search for her, calling her by name, but there was neither sight nor sound of her.

Then, in the distance, on the shore, lit up by the moonlight and starlight both, a figure approached.

"Joy," I said inwardly, relieved that she had come at last.

But as the figure moved near, there was something strange and strikingly unfamiliar about her movement. And then, behind her, another figure, then another, and yet another. I turned to move away, but there I saw them all the more: On the other side of me, another figure approached, followed by a mob of shadows. I looked feverishly for a way out, but from everywhere I looked, I saw them approach.

"Joy!" I screamed out, believing now her rescue was my only hope.

Silence.

As the figures drew nearer, I began to recognize their shapes, one by one:

The two boys who had tormented me in Grade Two, teasing me with relentless cruelty every recess and lunch. There they were, before me now just as they were then.

The boy who had jumped me on the bus to school so many years ago, landing atop me, punching me brutally in the face. He too was here now, the same size and shape now as then.

There, in the distance, the high school professor whose dislike for me led him to embarrass me before an entire class.

There, on my right, people I loved, trapped in their moments of anger. Mom berating me for not taking better care of my sister. Dad exclaiming, "How could you?" My sister, enraged at my lack of caring.

I cowered, terrified by the angry mob approaching me this night. What had happened on my Island of Paradise? What had gone so terribly wrong?

Whatever it was that was happening, it was far beyond the understanding of my mind.

"Then look beyond that limited vision, and to the understanding of your soul," a thought spoke out boldly.

It not only seemed like a good idea at the time, it was my only idea at the time. I calmed my mind, and felt the Divinity of my breath. That opened a doorway to the understanding of my soul.

It was then that I heard it, a whisper at first, but then a calm, clear voice—the words of Joy. She was guiding me through this experience, just as she had guided me into this space.

"Look now at one of these people as they approach," she spoke in rhythms that calmed the racing of my heartbeat. "Look into their eyes."

There I saw her, Mom caught in an angry moment, her eyes awash in anger. I had done something terribly wrong.

"This is bad, this is very bad," I thought, an enraged mom approaching slowly. She stopped, five feet in the distance, fury coloring her face.

"Look into her eyes," Joy continued, "and experience her beyond the limiting visions of your judgment. Her anger is not bad, for each experience simply *is*. Her anger is no more or less beautiful than any other experience in your time on your Island of Paradise."

"How do I see it, Joy?" a scared part of me called out. A mom with anger painting her face seemed far worse than the gentle tides of water that I had walked through earlier this day.

"It is easy," Joy replied with calm reassurance. "Breathe deep and let the wonder of the words I will now share awake a wonder in your soul.

"Do you remember your sadness? We watched you learn it as a small child. We saw it help you stay out of a preschool you did not wish to attend.

"Do you remember your anger? We saw you use it to serve you. It was a tool to help you motivate a careless driver to operate with more caution."

I remembered these things just as Joy described them.

"In this moment, then," Joy continued, a voice of calm in the sea of fury that surrounded me, "see the anger in the face before you. See and understand why your mother stands here with this unhappy expression.

"She experiences anger because it is a tool she learned. Just as you used anger to motivate change in the driver, so your mother uses anger now to motivate you."

Yes, through the softness and confidence of Joy's words, I could begin to see that.

"There is no reason for fear," Joy offered with soothing clarity. "Your mother's anger, directed toward you, says nothing about your worth and nothing about your value." Each word now felt as if it came straight from Heaven. "All your mother's anger communicates is that she has found an unhappy way to try to motivate you."

My mom's anger said nothing about me. Strange as that sounded, when Joy said it, there was no doubt it had always been true. Her anger was just her tool.

"Your mother's anger hurts *her*," Joy declared, her tone turning soft, as she spoke in tones of compassion. "As she gets angry, she experiences her own anger. The angrier she gets at you, the deeper she falls into her own depths of despair. In the moments she is angry at you, she is hurting inside.

"Look into her eyes," Joy's voice beckoned. "See beyond the judgment of her anger as bad, for this supports your fear," she announced. "See, deep in your mother's eyes, just beyond the thin veil of anger, the pain she is experiencing as she is angry at you. She is in so much pain that she now lashes out, seeking to hurt you so that you will learn.

"See, through looking in her eyes," Joy continued, drawing

me deeper into visions of my mother, "the pain she is in when she lashes out at you with words. And, seeing her great pain, know within your heart compassion even greater."

"Yes, Joy, I feel it," I declared. "These people, my mom, all of them around me tonight, such great sadness and anger...all in such pain...using anger and sadness because it is the only tool they know.

"I'm here for you all," I declared, wanting to let them know that despite their anger, there was a person in this world who could see beyond its shallow surface and into the depths beyond. I could see the pain that lay just beneath their thin covering.

"Sweet one," Joy's guiding voice announced, a hint of celebration in its tone, "do you realize that which you have done?"

I had no idea.

"You have just lived beyond judgment," Joy announced with excitement. "Do you not see, in the face of an angry mob, all the people in your life who hurt you, all the people in your life that loved you caught in moments in which they were ready to hurt you...you have stopped seeing that experience as bad. You do not judge it anymore.

"You have seen beyond the eyes of judgment. Freed from that limiting vision, you have liberated yourself to respond with Love, and you have, through the wonder of your compassion."

"I did all that?" my mind wondered, as the realization dawned on me. "I did all that!" my soul shouted with glee, delighted that I was at last living as she would have me live.

I looked around me now, taking in the figures on the sandy shore of the Island of Paradise. This was a land once again living up to its name.

Now, surrounding me in a circle five feet in radius, were people who throughout my life directed their anger and sadness toward me. There were those that had loved me deeply, caught in moments when they had forgotten, and there were those who, it had seemed to me, had spent all our time together in an attempt to hurt.

I looked at them now, feeling nothing but compassion for these people. Their anger and sadness had not been my punishment, although through the limiting eyes of judgment I had called it bad and experienced it that way. Rather, something far more magnificent was in play here. Beyond the limitations of judgments, I saw what was and had always been there to see: people in pain, and from the place of pain and fear, doing the best they knew how.

I saw the depths of their pain, so deep they sought to hurt me too, and I felt only the greatest of compassion for each and every one of them then. In that moment, I had transcended my judgment, and responded with the Love that I was.

Suddenly, to my surprise, the circle of angry and sad people around me broke into a collective smile. Big, broad, red brush strokes of pleasure colored their faces!

I joined in, caught up in the moment, wondering what had caused this sudden wellspring of wonder.

"You see them now as they truly are," Joy's words explained without my asking, "and you see their sadness and their anger as it was always meant to be seen. You have understood the truth beyond your fear.

"Never forget that which you have learned tonight. To see beyond the limiting vision of judgment is to see with the soul, and to see with the soul, why, that is to live fully."

With those words, I felt myself float up off my inner island paradise, and up into the night sky. I knew my time here was up, and this was the beginning of my journey homeward.

I floated now away from the Island of Paradise. As she became but a distant memory, I swear I heard her whisper, "You are welcome back here any time of your choosing."

I floated upward now, higher and higher into the night sky, until at last I saw a star summoning me. I floated upward, and upward still, as she grew in size, her greeting to me. The star's light quickly dwarfed a night sky, and soon I was embraced by her softness.

I was carried by her wonder though a tunnel of warmth, and released gently into my body, now stiff from its time on the living room floor.

I awoke myself gently, with slow and circular movements, and, upon awakening my body, opened my eyes. There, aglow on my living room couch was Joy, beaming.

I smiled back, delighted by memories of my journey.

Suddenly, a thought jumped up through my mind, and I shared her with Joy. "Why, in the middle of that night on the Island of Paradise, did you leave me?"

"Sweet one," Joy offered with unimaginable gentleness. "I shall never leave you. It is only that you must remember where to look in order to find me. For I spend far more time within than with-out."

With that, she arose, said a soft goodbye, walked ever so softly down the stairwell and out the front door, and left me to my newfound awareness.

Chapter 24

Bringing Tools to Life

In the days that followed my Saturday with Joy, I discovered a world previously unknown to me.

I walked down city streets, a rush of people hurrying by. I had passed this way a thousand times before. But on this day, the Routine of the Scene transformed herself into a Dance of Delight.

The people I walked by, very much the same in outward appearance, looked very different when seen through the new lenses of my internal world.

Once, not so long ago, people on the street were no different than carbon cutouts, obstacles in my path to be avoided. But today, I slowed my pace, taking in a vision of each person I passed by.

I could see past the painted faces each hid behind. There, just beneath a thin exterior, was a sweet soul doing the best she knew how in her life.

The anger and the sadness that shaped so many faces now framed a new vision. Once, each pained expression was a reflection of my imperfection (they must be unhappy with me) and a statement of their fallacy (what's the matter with them that they can't just smile). Once, their sadness was a testament to the sorry state of our world (a world filled with so much misery).

Today, their sadness and their anger became the best these beings knew to do to care for themselves. Just as I had used anger and sadness as tools, so too did they now.

With this new vision, I filled myself with compassion for their self-inflicted misery. I experienced newfound acceptance and allowance for them just as they were, and felt a love for my fellow man that I had always said I wanted, but until this day had never experienced.

My new vision brought me more peace on a city street that day than I had known even in the comfort of home.

But despite the profound visions unfolding before my eyes, my soul knew I was but a newborn babe on my journey to wonder. She invited me to stack the odds in my favor. "Create and maintain an environment that best supports your well-being," she declared.

Soul's thought in my mind, I walked the wonder of city streets and returned to the mystical Land of Paradigm. It was there that the gentle sounds she sang to me through her loudspeakers had calmed my soul, and it was there that the sweet smell of sandalwood incense had put my body at ease. This time, rather than a search through her landscape for a new book to enliven my spirit, I took her soothing sounds and smells home with me, buying both audiotape and incense. I welcomed into my home the sensations that were a calming influence in what I knew could feel like a world of anxiety.

While my mind insisted I could make it on my own, my soul knew the challenges and pitfalls of living joy when surrounded by a world of self-inflicted misery. "We will only live joy," my soul declared, "when you remember you want to live with joy. Bring the Invention of Intention to life in your everyday."

Listening to the knowing of my soul, I was excited by the blueprint she laid out for living the task at hand. "Turn everyday events into spiritual ones," became my soul's new mantra. "Rather than wait for the annual arrival of Christmas to remember the spirit that you want alive in your daily life, empower everyday experiences to become your personal Christmases."

First was the ringing phone. I never picked up a phone again until her third ring, using her first two to trigger and ignite my intention to live with joy. Every phone call became a living reminder that joy was what I wanted most of all.

It continued with traffic lights. I traded in the frustration I encountered with the sea of red light that painted my way. I declared each stop a new time to fire myself up with the intention of joy.

The possibilities for empowering everyday events were endless. Before I knew it, the spectrum of routine daily experiences were suddenly empowering my journey to joy, bringing the Invention of Intention aglow in my life.

Remembering I wanted joy in the moments of my life was a wondrous first step. Surrounded by a sea of colleagues prioritizing work at the expense of personal joy and well-being, I used the Invention of Intention, and all the newly empowered everyday experiences, to remember: my joy was never worth surrendering.

Remembering was one thing. Living what I remembered was quite another.

"There are only two things coming your way in this life," my soul began, reminding me of Joy's wisdom, "either you shall get that which you want, or you shall get that which you do not want.

"Getting that which you want shall present no obstacles to your joy. Getting that which you do not, and maintaining Joy, shall require a life beyond judgment."

"The key for you is in the asking," my soul spoke in riddles. Clarifying, she explained the wisdom of her words. "Whenever adversity comes your way, ask questions, this time not as indictments, but rather to create opportunity. Trade in, 'Why is this happening to me?' and 'What's wrong with this world?' Replace these with, 'Is my well-being really worth giving up over this?' and 'What part of myself do I wish to call forth now?' Use your Invention of Intention, alive now in everyday experience, to answer, 'No, my well-being is never worth giving up, for she is my highest calling,' and, 'That which I wish to experience is my compassion for my hardship and my passion for creating the life of my dreams.' "

Suddenly, questions, once a tool to incriminate and indict, came to life in an empowering way. With Intention firmly in the grasp of one hand, and the daring to ask questions that invited the knowing of my intention in the other, I was a two-fisted wonder.

I was not a living example of joy in *all* moments of my life that week, but I started giving myself the gift of my living joy in more moments than I thought possible just the week before.

I couldn't wait for the next Saturday with Joy to learn all the more that I could find within my joy everlasting.

Saturday

February 16

Chapter 25

The Difference of Persistence

I awoke early on Saturday, my body pleading for more rest. But mind conspired with soul, and together they woke my body despite her cries. "It's Saturday!" the thoughts in my mind shouted. "Joy's coming!" my soul exclaimed.

It had been a wondrous week, filled with my intention to create joy, and my new practice of life beyond the illusion of judgment. I had, for the first week in a long time, begun to live my dream of a lifetime of happiness.

For the longest time, I had pointed an accusatory finger at my work and my relationships, blaming them for the misery I felt. To my surprise, I now found my liberation by changing the direction in which that finger pointed, and in transforming its accusatory nature. Now I directed that finger inward, and rather than accusation, I sought understanding.

I moved through my home, my thoughts revisiting and rejoicing in the events and transformations of the week gone by. Following morning routine, my body moved unguided into the kitchen, mixing together the two ingredients that formed my breakfast bowl of cereal. Bowl in one hand, body ventured down the stairs to the front door where it gathered my morning paper. My body moved at last to the living room couch, where it sat itself down victoriously, bowl in right hand, paper in my left. It invited my mind to return and rejoice in what it had gathered together.

My mind ventured back from its journey to a world of praise and accolades for a week fully lived, and began to give its attention to the food before me and the headlines that colored the morning paper.

"What the...?" my voice shouted, as my body jumped and my mind raced. A spoon full of cereal crashed to the floor. Someone was beside me on the couch.

"Joy!" I shouted angrily, my mind quickly identifying the size and shape of the body by my side, and soul recognizing the warm glow of radiance that was unmistakably Joy.

Silence was Joy's only response. As my mind took her in, I saw now that she was sitting in a meditative pose, legs crossed in full lotus position, back straight, eyes closed. She was lost to the world around her, and alive to a hidden world within.

"Why is Joy suddenly beside me meditating?" one thought piped out inquisitively. "She didn't suddenly appear," a collective of neighboring thoughts spoke in reply, realizing the reality of the moment, "you've been lost in our world of thinking, and you missed Joy all the while she sat aglow on the living room couch." She hadn't suddenly appeared, she'd been here all morning. She hadn't scared me, I'd scared myself.

"What now?" I wondered, an image of spilled cereal, morning paper, and meditative Joy before me. I decided not to think much about it, instead trusting what I knew to do. I cleaned up the cereal that had dropped to the floor. Next, I sat and ate, curbing my morning hunger while delighting in the image of Joy. I had hoped Joy would return from her meditative state so that we could begin our time together. But still she sat, a radiant fixture on my living room couch. I turned to the newspaper, deciding to read while awaiting Joy's return from her internal adventure.

Soon, I had read all I was ready to take in, and still Joy sat, an image of silence and serenity. I thought about waking Joy from her state of being, thinking she had intended to return but accidentally lost herself in her internal landscape. While my mind mounted a case for her arousal, my soul knew that something all together different was to go on here.

I listened to the calling of my soul. "If she is not to come to you, then you must go to her," soul announced. "Sit beside Joy, follow her lead," soul beckoned.

When I tried to sit as Joy did, my body mounted a protest: "These legs don't bend in *that* way, and this back will hurt when you do *this*." In an attempt to placate both body and soul, my mind guided me to the bedroom; I took two pillows, and returned to the couch. I placed them both beneath me, elevating my back, and my body now agreed to sit just as Joy did, thanks to a little help from two soft friends.

I closed my eyes, sitting now in both silence and darkness, Joy by my side. My mind argued, "There must be something to do here," but my soul knew the paradox of the place: "Doing nothing is the best there is to do." I repeated Joy's words of guidance: "Nowhere to go, and nothing to do. There never has been. There never will be." As I heard those words again, my body relaxed, my mind quieted, and my soul felt strangely alive.

I sat now, quietly, feeling the gentle tides of my breath, as thought floated by much like clouds on a sunshine day. The longer I sat, the clearer the sky became, and soon I felt only the tides of breath swaying in an ocean of wonder. I radiated from the inside out. Time lost her meaning. I felt alive in a sea of delight, shimmering with reflections of a light from deep within.

I saw then a vision of myself, perched high on a boulder mounted on a rocky shore, watching the beauty of my internal world. I looked out over an Ocean of Wonder, my awareness of a Living Body. I saw above her a sun aglow with the light of my Soul.

Then I heard her beside me, as sure and soft and ever, "Hello, sweet one, it is wondrous to be with you again." It was Joy, speaking to me in a way that felt deeper than words.

"Joy, I'm so glad to see you," I said, my voice revealing my heart's profound love for her presence.

"Sweet one, you have taken giant steps this week, and you have reaped the rewards of your efforts.

"But there is still much you wish to learn, and my time with you is getting short. So please, dear one, ask that which you most want to know."

For a moment, I most wanted to know what she meant by "her time with me was getting short," but deep within I knew these were times where great insights were possible, and questions more pressing and profound jumped me then.

"Joy," I began, "this week I entered the world and spent time, at last, living joy from within. But still, there were so many moments when I was inconsistent, when I forgot despite all my Inventions of Intention to live with joy. How do you do it? How do you live delight in *every* moment?"

"Sweet one," Joy began, "the answer to this is that which you already know. This you have known for a long time indeed. It is the Difference of Persistence.

"Life," Joy continued, "is simply a collection of moments. And each moment is but an invitation.

"Each moment appears, asking of you only one question: 'Would you like to manifest Joy in this moment?' You may answer yes just as you are free to answer no.

"Then," Joy spoke, her words calming and confident, "if you do not choose Joy in one moment, the next moment appears as a newborn child, asking you naught but the very same thing, 'Would you like Joy in this moment?' Again, you are free to answer as you would choose.

"Life, in her infinite patience, provides you with but a never-ending series of moments, and in each one you are free to choose: Joy or not.

"Creating joy is *not* a practice where in one moment, like a light bulb suddenly switching on, you understand how to create joy, and in every moment thereafter you live joy. And thank goodness creating joy is not this way—for in this way there would be no free will and no free choice after that first moment of enlightening awareness.

"Rather, joy *is* a constant act of creation. She is there for you to create in your every moment.

"The more you shall practice creating joy, the easier she shall become to create. It is like learning to drive a car.

"At first driving is hard, for you do not know just how to use brake and accelerator and steering wheel. You get in and you drive, and as you gain familiarity, it becomes easier and easier.

"Soon, you are driving down the streets, on your way to wherever you wish, and driving a car is but second nature. You no longer need to think about it, for it is in you. It is just what you do.

"Joy is that very same way. Practice her, be persistent, live the Difference of Persistence, and she will become just that which you know to do. And life will be a journey of sheer delight.

"But there are no guarantees in this life. In each moment, just as you may crash a car into a wall if you are not paying enough attention to that which you do, so, too, is it this way with joy. You shall crash her into a wall of misery if you stop being persistent in your practice of her.

"There is only the practice of joy, and being persistent in her practice. The more persistent you are, the more easily will you find yourself choosing her, and the more moments shall you spend in her abundance."

And with those words, Joy spun a story that formed a web of wonder:

> Once, in a time not long ago, and in a place not far away, there lived two beings. Both had lost their way to the land of joy, and both cried out to the heavens: "I shall find my way to joy, no matter the cost, regardless the risk. For joy is my birthright, and I shall reclaim that which is rightfully mine."
>
> The first being set out the very next day on a journey to joy.
>
> Wanting to help the first being on her way, the Universe offered the being adversity. The Universe hoped the being would see that she could be joyful even in the face of hardship.
>
> But the being was unable to create her joy in moments of adversity. Deciding this was a sign of

failure, the being felt within the experience of frustration.

It was then that she shouted out, "Oh, would you look at me! I declare how much I want Joy, screaming it to the heavens, and yet adversity comes along the very next day and immediately I lose my way."

"This proves it," the being announced, continuing her downward spiral, "I shall never find my way to the land of Joy."

Allowing her words to become a self-fulfilling prophecy, the being abandoned her journey to joy right there and then, declaring, "All that I shall find on this route is my own disappointment."

The second being, watching the experience of the first, decided she would walk to joy in an altogether different way.

As the second being began her journey joy-ward, the Universe, in an effort to support her, decided to throw adversity her way. The Universe intended to teach her that she could maintain joy even in the face of hardship.

But alas, as with the first, the experience of adversity was too great for the second being. In the face of it, she too felt frustration.

However, carrying the Difference of Persistence with her, the second being responded to her frustration in an altogether different way.

"Yes, I got frustrated," she declared to herself and her Universe, "but I will speak in response but a few words: 'No big deal.'

"Life will be filled with moments, and in each moment I shall have a chance to decide anew how I feel. There shall be moments, surely, in this life, that I shall experience the turmoil of frustration and the hardships of anger and sadness.

"What is important is not that these moments happen, but how I respond when they do. In saying, 'No big deal,' I invite myself to let go of my moments of misery, and not build them into mountains of madness.

"With 'No big deal,' I free myself from the shackles of sadness, and can decide anew in the next moment that which I want: my joy."

And so when adversity came her way, and the second being chose not to offer herself the wonder of her joy, she simply declared, 'No big deal,' and let go of her moments of misery.

In the moments that followed her misery, she persisted in seeking her joy, and it was in this way that she quickly reclaimed the gifts of her wonder.

Soon, in more and more moments of adversity, the being was responding naught but with joy. In these instances, she rewarded herself with accolades of praise and words of congratulations. "Way to go!" she would declare. "You go, girl!" she exclaimed.

And so it was, the second being never abandoned her journey to joy. And so it was as it must be. The second being found her way back to her birthright of magnificence.

And all she achieved she received for but one reason: the Difference of Persistence.

We sat in silence for a time, Joy and I, on a boulder that looked out over my internal landscape. Ocean reflected the sunlight of my soul.

"Do you see now, sweet one?" Joy offered softly, breaking our silence. "Persist and you shall surely have that which you most want.

"Nurture persistence," she continued, in gentle tones and easy rhythms, her voice a reflection of the perfect world that lay before us now. "Celebrate in the face of creating joy. Give no mind when you choose another way. For that which you give your attention to, that shall you make bigger."

We sat for a long time in silence. There was no hurry here in this place beyond space and time.

"Just like everything else," I said, speaking at last, "practice makes perfect."

"No, sweet one," Joy offered in reply, speaking slowly and highlighting each word as if it were more important than the one before, "you are already perfect. Just as you are. All there ever is to do is practice seeing and living your perfection.

"You have taken the illusion of lack-of-divinity and practiced it into your perception of reality. Now, as always, you are free to open the same doorway. With practice and persistence, you are free to return to the truth from whence you came."

"I'm always hoping that there'll be an easy way," I noted, "the wave of a magic wand to take me from here to there, from where I am to everlasting joy."

"Sweet child," Joy spoke, again softness filling her voice, "as we have said before, there are no magic wands, for they would rid you of your personal power to create that which you most want.

"You may journey a long road or a short one to get from that which is where you are to that which is where you want to be," Joy continued. "The length of that journey is up to you, measured only by the depth of your intention and persistence."

Chapter 26

The Attitude of Gratitude

W hatever lengths you travel," Joy continued, "when your journey is to joy, be sure to remember this. In each moment that you look to see where it is you are, and regardless of where you find yourself then, be content with your place. Always enjoy all there is in life at the moment of looking."

I looked at Joy, a puzzled expression coloring my face.

"Just as you have forgotten your perfection, so too have you forgotten how to walk the roads of your life seeing the perfection in the journey.

"You have decided that you must *get there* at all costs, believing *getting there* will prove your worth and value. You are so caught up in arriving, you forget to look around you while on the journey, for, if you did, the delight in what surrounded you would light up the moments of your life."

And with that Joy turned to her storytelling ways, speaking in parables the magic of her words:

Once upon a time, and what a time it was, there lived a village of creatures. Each creature in the village did not believe in the wonder and the worth that they were. They had forgotten the divinity that was their birthright.

But there was one born among them who had not forgotten. She knew the wonder that she was. Those around her counseled her, imploring her to live the ways of the village. "There must be something wrong with you," they declared. Indictments disguised as questions were asked of her, with the hope of showing her the error of her thinking: "How dare you think you are perfect just as you are?" they inquired. "What right do you have to think the universe made you perfect?" they asked.

But despite the pressures to conform to the Illusion of Imperfection, the creature remained firm in the truth of who she was. Often she traveled to the nearby mountainsides, seeking solitude from the madness that infected her village. For the mountains, in their grandeur, knew the truth of perfection in all living things.

One day, in the village, there grew among them a rumor that high on a mountainside lived a Flower of Power, and all who saw her would know joy everlasting.

As the rumor spread, a meeting was called, and the villagers gathered together. They decided to elect among them the best of climbers to go and seek that which it was they wanted to find.

It came to pass that the best climber among them was she who knew of her perfection.

And she who knew of her perfection said, "I should be delighted to take this walk for you, and seek this Flower of Power, that you might have that which you want. For I love naught but to climb the heights of the mountain tops, for it is there that I am closest to God."

The villagers did not understand all that she said.

"But if she will climb the mountain tops and return with the Flower of Power, what does it matter whether we understand her," the villagers said to one another. And so they gave her all the provisions they could muster, and sent her on a long journey to the heights of the mountains, to find the Flower of Power.

Unsure they could trust one so strange as she, on a mission so important as this, they sent a second villager out behind her, he who would keep an eye on her.

ᴥ   ᴥ   ᴥ

The creature-of-perfection headed out on her way, followed by the one-who-would-shadow-her-journey. The creature-of-perfection knew there was no hurry, no rush, for all things came in the time they were ready. She would be sure, now as always, to delight in her journey, to create it as perfect, just as she was perfect.

And so it was as she climbed the mountainside, she stopped and delighted in the fresh smell of the wildflowers. She spent time lying on the earth, watching the visions of the passing clouds drift their way by, each shaped in ever-changing ways, as was all life. She stopped to listen to the sweet sounds of the songbirds, chirping tunes of gratitude for the gift of life. She stopped to taste the flow of fresh water that cascaded down the mountainside. All the while, she continued on her way, delighting in each moment of her journey.

He who followed her marveled at her ways, for as he too did as she did, he began to feel a delight in the wonder of life that he had not felt before. He began to see a perfection around him, and began to feel a perfection alive in him.

At last, she arrived at the tops of the mountains, and there she saw a red rose, as was described to her in the village hall. "This," she wondered to herself, "this is the Flower of Power? For she is wondrous indeed, wondrous and perfect in her wonder as is all life, but there is nothing mystical about her. She is no more mystical than the clouds in the sky, nor the sounds of the songbird, nor the taste of the mountain water."

And he who followed her, stood beside her now, pondering this very same thing.

❧   ❧   ❧

Then they heard it, the voice of the Flower of Power speaking to them, as all things speak to us when only we learn to listen.

"Your villagers," the flower began, speaking with the gentleness that only a rose could, "cannot yet delight in the wonder of that which I am. For they see not the wonder of the world around them, nor the wonder that lies within them.

"I cannot be cut down and returned to your village," the rose explained, "for there they will say I am naught but an ordinary rose, just as they will say they are naught but ordinary villagers.

"Rather, invite your villagers to journey to me. On their journey, they are free in any moment to stop and look around at the abundance of life that surrounds. When they do, they will see, as they look with eyes open wide, the wonder of all life. They shall see then this as a reflection of the wonder that they are.

"Joy is in the search, not only the finding; the beauty in the walk, not only in its ending."

᪥   ᪥   ᪥

And so it was that she-who-knew-her-perfection, and he-who-had-followed, who knew his wonder now as well, came down the mountainside. Returning to the village, they reported all that they had heard and seen, hoping to inspire the villagers to seek out the Flower of Power themselves, and discover their joy in the journey.

But the villagers were enraged, and cast out she-who-knew-her-perfection and he-who-now-knew-his-too. "These are traitors to our village," it was declared, "selfish souls who knew not how to give their people that which they most wanted. Had they not been told to bring back the Flower of Power?"

So it came to pass that she and he who knew the secret of the Flower spent a life together delighting in the wonder of all that is, away from a village once called home.

Meanwhile, for years without end, the villagers sent out search parties, scouring the mountainsides with hopes of finding the Flower of Power. They climbed the mountainside with machetes in hand, cutting down all that was in their way. They walked with their heads down, never stopping to see the beauty that called to them from all around. They grumbled and filled themselves with misery, talking of how terrible and awful the entire journey was, and how they could not wait to get to their destination.

From these villagers did the Flower of Power hide herself, never to be found by them, for true wonder was in the journey, not in the finding.

"Joy, how do you make the road you walk a joyful one in any moment? Why is it, in your story, the first person was able to walk and see the wonder of life, while the others couldn't?"

"The difference is in the remembering," Joy began, her voice a blend of calm and confidence. "It is to remember this. *Slow down.*

"Slow down your journey to wherever it is you are going. Slow down enough that you would have moments where you could stop and look around you. For life is filled with beauty. But you rush to get *there* so fast that all you see is a blur of color, and you miss the beauty in the detail of life.

"For I tell you this: The Universe, in every moment, seeks to support you in your journey to reclaiming your vision of perfection. She surrounds you with an unending supply of gifts to aid.

"But you miss the gifts of the Universe, sometimes one and sometimes all, because you walk through life head down, concerned only with your destination. In so doing, you miss the support offered to help you get to where you wish to go.

"You can learn to see the support of your Universe, catching glimpses of her loving kindness nurturing you in your every moment.

"With the Attitude of Gratitude, you shall see visions of the support offered to you by the Universe.

"The Attitude of Gratitude is the invitation to slow down, slow down enough to see that which you have in any moment, and *celebrate* that.

"As you slow down and begin to see the abundance in any moment, you are no longer able to deny that the Universe is holding you in her soft caress. You can now see her supporting you every step of your way in your walk to reclaiming your vision of Divinity. With gratitude, you shall see and feel this.

"Many know of gratitude, yet they do not invite it into their lives. They fear that the Attitude of Gratitude declares, 'Abandon getting to where you are going, and just delight in the wonder of now.' But this is not her wisdom. Rather, gratitude announces, 'Journey to where it is you wish to go, and along the way revel in the wonder of where you are, ever-changing as it may be.'

"She-who-knew-her-perfection journeyed to the Flower of Power while celebrating in all of life along the way. Indeed, she never would have found her destination had she not. So too can you delight in all the abundance that your world affords you, while walking your way through life."

I sat on the boulder of my internal landscape, Joy by my side, looking out at a vast ocean that lay before me. Thoughts mounted a rebellion, banding together to counter Joy's words of gratitude. "They sound too good. Too simple. There's something not quite right here," my thoughts declared. I shared their grumblings.

"Let's face it, Joy," my thoughts piped out, "there's just too much misery in my world to enjoy what I've got."

"Please, tell me more, dear one," Joy spoke, inviting me to continue.

"Don't you read the headlines, Joy? No, I suppose you don't.

"Damn it, Joy, the world's going mad. There are people killing people every day. There are people killing themselves every day. There are wars raging all over this planet, where people fire weapons of mass destruction and commit murder by the hundreds: for a piece of land here and a bit of control there. There are acts of genocide, people wiping out entire populations because they don't like what others believe or how they look. People are so scared, they hide themselves behind locked doors and electric fences and alarm systems. The first thing we teach our children is don't talk to strangers. As if killing and terrorizing ourselves were not enough, we mass murder animals, we destroy natural habitats and we wipe out entire ecosystems.

"And you want me to be grateful, to see what I have and how wonderful it all is. Come on, Joy! Maybe I can find my way to joy, but there is no way I'm going to sugarcoat the world to make it happen."

"Sweet one," Joy said, with such softness that just those words began to soothe my teeming thoughts, "you are always welcome to see the world in this way. It is neither a good nor a bad way to see the world, it is just one way.

"However, it is a way that, as is apparent to you and me both, will not support your ability to live with joy. There is an altogether different way to look at this very same world."

I sat, calmed by Joy's words, and her willingness to accept mine. I was ready to hear Joy's way. But as I waited, she sat in silence.

"Joy," I declared, "aren't you going to tell me this new way to see the world?" I imagined her inspirational words helping me live with unbounded gratitude.

"No," she replied gently.

"No!" I exclaimed. "What do you mean, *'No'?*"

"Why don't you tell me the new way to see the world?" Joy invited. "It is alive in you now, a small seed ready to grow. You tell me."

Joy turned her words into guidance. "Close your eyes. Go

within. Listen to the knowing of your soul that lives just beneath the illusion of judgment that clouds your mind."

I closed my eyes. Calmed myself with deep breaths. Opened my eyes to the view of ocean and sunshine alive above. The beauty with-out inspired my beauty within. Words that had been locked inside for what felt like all time, suddenly burst through.

"This world celebrates herself with the beauty of a sunrise every morning," I began, my excited tone inspired by my words. "The sunrise paints the sky in celebration of the coming day. In the moments following her morning call, people come to life. Unseen to the eyes of many, unreported in the morning paper, the miracle of life begins anew, filled with hope and possibility for the day dawning.

"People support each other. Each day is filled with small acts of great love. The acts are so small they pass the notice of many a passerby. But to those touched by the act of kindness, the acts are great indeed. And there are not one, not ten, not one hundred, not one million of these acts, but countless numbers each day.

"The day comes to a close, celebrating the wonder and perfection of life with a sunset, a vision of blazing color for all to behold, a perfect ending to what could be nothing but a beautiful day.

"Sure, there are many things that I want different in the world, each and every day, and I would be blind if I didn't see their presence. These are the acts caused by well-intentioned people living through fear.

"I am free to rage against the world for the presence of things I don't like, but that does nothing but create another unhappy person on the planet. I am also free to work to create the planet that I want. As I do this, I give myself the experience of the best that I am.

"At no point along the way do I ever have to abandon my joy. I can embrace the world around me, seeing all there is to celebrate, touching the abundance of life, feeling the gratitude for this gift, and all the while I can work to create the world I want to be a part of."

It was as if those words had been trapped within for a millennium, and at last they had burst forth. I was stunned and at the same time energized by the wisdom that flowed through me.

"Wondrous," Joy shared in response. "Now come that you might experience that which we have shared." With that, she took me by the hand, and together we drifted up into the blue sky.

As we floated upward, I saw her, alive even in the day-lit sky: a star, small yet twinkling. It was as if she had refused to leave with her brothers and sisters, awaiting our arrival, knowing we would come to her on this day. She called us to her, and we flew toward her beckoning. Soon, we were high in the day sky, and the once-small star above us grew into a brilliant white light, filling space with the warmth of her possibility.

In moments we entered into her welcoming embrace, and she transformed herself into a tunnel of light. I could feel a slow movement through the doorway of time. Yet there was something strange about this journey.

"We are moving forward through time, into that which might be," Joy announced, answering my unspoken wondering.

Soon, the tunnel gave way to its end, and it was then that she released us ever so gently into the future that might be. There was a flash of light, and then I saw it.

Chapter 27

Marriage

My eyes adjusted quickly to the changing light, and I began to piece together the scene unfolding before me. We were outdoors, in the openness of bright blue sky. An occasional white cloud wandered her way by.

Joy and I sat, side by side, beneath an archway overflowing with the greens and whites of flowers that called this wooden structure home.

Through the archway where we sat, a long white carpet flowed.

On each side of the carpet sat rows of chairs, one after another, seating perhaps fifty. The chairs were filled with people of all shapes and sizes, dressed in all colors of the rainbow. The men dressed mostly in black, their Sunday best suits. Multi-colored ties fell downward from their collars, coloring the whites of their shirts. The women expressed themselves with far more vibrancy, in dresses painted bright reds, soft yellows, baby blues and patterned whites.

The white carpet flowed gently through these rows of people, leading center-stage, where a small wooden structure greeted her. The white wood was overgrown with a green ivy covering nearly its entire body. Beneath the structure stood a man dressed in his long-tailed tux, long curly hair an explosion of black on the top of his head. A goatee shaped his face, a bow tie and vest painted the many shades of purple colored his suit, and a glow from deep within colored his expression. He looked toward the archway where we sat, as if waiting for something.

My mind pieced together the imagery sent its way. This was a wedding, a small outdoor summer wedding. But whose? I studied the groom far more carefully now, and the more I looked at his face, the more certain I became. That man in the front was me! This was *my* wedding!

"I wonder who I'm marrying," I thought to myself.

As if in reply to my curiosity, three musicians began to sing just then, their vocals, lyrics and guitars a ray of sunshine for the soul. Suddenly, the groom's eyes lit up, and, as I watched, I was sure I saw his heart skip a beat. I had never before seen delight paint a face as fully as it did his in that moment.

Everyone turned to look behind them. I turned, too, and it was then I saw her.

I have seen many beautiful women in my life, but none, not ever, quite like this one. She was a vision of absolute marvel. Deep blue eyes were a living testament to the depth of her soul. Long dark blond hair cascaded gracefully onto her shoulders. Flowers were tied into the curls spun by her hair, as if, captivated by her beauty, the flowers had jumped in, that they too might be a part of her wonder. A white wedding dress covered the delicate shapes of her body, and an explosion of pink and white flowers sat gracefully in her hands.

A father beaming by her side, she walked down the aisle, gliding gently past Joy and I. The groom shared a broad smile with her as she approached, and she responded in kind, sharing with him the fullness of her pleasure. Soon they stood side by side, filling center stage with their delight.

Something magical was taking place before my eyes. Something beyond the wedding scene that played itself out before me then. Something deeper. I had never seen anything quite like this before. Two people alive to the wonder of each moment. As they stood, a spectacle of love for all to see, they played gently with the shapes of each other's hands, marveling in the softness of their shared touch. They heard the minister's tales of unconditional love and shared a soft smile when words touched their hearts. They looked out together to the aisles of people who filled the seats and shared with them their expressions of pleasure, a thank you for being a part of this celebration.

They were married that day. But in every moment along the way, they were alive with a joy and a marvel for each moment.

I understood then the wisdom of gratitude: Move toward what you want, all the while delighting in the wonder of the abundance that surrounds.

It was then that Joy offered me her hand. I took its gentle embrace, and again we headed heavenward toward the sunlit sky. There, our star sat patiently, awaiting our return. As we flew upward toward her, she welcomed us with her light. Soon we were warmed by her gentle embrace, and we traveled her doorways back to the time I called home. When her light gave way to its end, I felt the easy rhythms of my breath, and the aches of a body left seated on the living room couch, two pillows supporting it in a full lotus position.

I moved my body slowly, reawakening to the presence of my mind and soul. Soon, I opened my eyes, expecting Joy by my side. But she was gone, leaving as suddenly and mysteriously as she came. Another Saturday with Joy had come to a close.

Chapter 28

Living Joy

Armed with the Invention of Intention, ready to see beyond the illusions of judgment, and now, equipped with Difference of Persistence and the Attitude of Gratitude, I was ready to embrace my world.

Once, I walked city streets with frowns of despair covering my face. I saw a world I no longer liked and regretted that I lived in the midst of her.

Now, with the eyes of gratitude, I saw altogether different visions. A mother held her little boy's hand, offering him words of comfort as he complained of cold winter air. Friends walked city streets together, laughing and smiling as they shared stories of times gone by. A couple held hands and looked warmly at one another, sharing a secret moment of bliss. A man helped a teenager, her baby in a carriage, maneuver her way up a flight of stairs. When I opened my eyes to it, there was a world of miracle and wonder.

While city streets could paint pictures of the best of our world, they were also filled with images of her at her worst. An elderly man stood at a street corner, his face painted the color of sadness and his body disfigured by his time at war. He implored people to share with him the extras that filled their pockets.

Rather than sadness or rage at the world for the plight of this soul, I looked beyond the illusion of judgment. "What part of myself did I want to call forth in the face of this?" I asked myself. Compassion was first to jump to mind. I walked by the man whose cries for spare change were background noise to the city street. I practiced feeling my acceptance and allowance of him right where he was. This, like all of us, was a person doing the best he knew how to take care of himself in that moment. I could embrace him with an open heart right there and then, just as he was.

Each experience that week became opportunity. In seeing the abundance surrounding me, I celebrated the magnificence of the world. In seeing the world act out in ways I didn't want, I practiced a life beyond the illusion of judgment and learned to experience the best that I was.

I began to understand more profoundly now than ever before what Joy had meant when she shared: Each moment is the invitation, "Do you want happiness here with me?" In every moment, I could embrace the world that surrounded, just as I was free to bemoan it. In any moment, I was free to experience the best of who I was, just as I was free to experience myself at my very worst.

With intention, I remembered the invitation of my moments. It was an invitation I didn't always accept each time it came knocking.

But the times when I chose an experience very different than my joy, I practiced the words, "No big deal." They liberated me to choose joy in the moments that followed my misery.

When I did choose joy, accepting my moment's invitation with arms open wide, I celebrated the magnificence of that choice, cheerleading myself toward a life of wonder.

Saturday

February 23

Chapter 29

Beginnings and Endings

Saturday arrived again, and, much like the many before her, the coming of Joy was such excitement to mind and soul that they awoke body well before she was ready. With an alarm shining 6:30, and the darkness of winter still covering the sky, I moved my body out of bed, my mind and soul proclaiming Joy's coming.

I walked to the kitchen and started pouring myself a bowl of cereal. It was then I heard it, a loud knock on the door.

"Joy!" my soul cried out, certain it was her.

I abandoned breakfast, hurried out of the kitchen and down the entranceway stairs, and flung open the door with energy and enthusiasm. Sure enough, there she stood, as radiant and as wondrous as the first time she had appeared at my doorstep, a time that seemed now so long ago, and an experience that felt now so far away.

"Joy!" I exclaimed, excited by her presence.

"Sweet one," she replied, a smile dancing across her face, "what a difference now than the first time I came to your door."

"Yes," I said, beaming a broad smile. "I love you, Joy!" I announced, sharing the warm feelings that filled my insides every time I saw her.

"And I love you, dear one," she said, a soft and gentle reply. "I have loved you from before time began, and I shall love you beyond the ends of time."

"Wow, Joy, that sounds great!"

"However, dear one," Joy spoke with a sudden quietness in her voice, "this shall be the last time, in a long time, that I shall see you in this form."

"What do you mean?" I said, concern covering my face. Soul knew just what she meant, but mind was not yet ready to accept it.

"I mean that next Saturday you shall be creating joy without me. You are ready now to create joy on your own, and soon you shall fill your life with others who shall bring you wisdom and joy. My time with you in this form will be done for now, after our one final and most delicious journey on this day."

"But...when will I see you again?"

"Sweet one, do you not see? Nothing ends and nothing dies. Not now. Not ever.

"I shall live always inside of you, nurturing your soul from within. All that there ever is to do is turn to the wisdom of your soul, and there shall you find me. And there shall you find all that you wish. For within you lies far more than ever you could imagine, and the visions that you see with me now are but the foothills to the high peaks of glory that live in your soul."

Her words were calming and soothing, and I felt myself comforted by their love. But still, there was one thing I dearly wanted to know.

"Joy," I announced, "*when* will I ever see you in this form again?"

"I do not know," she offered gently.

"Now come," she announced with far more confidence, "there is a very important journey that we are to take on this day, a most wonderful of Saturdays."

With that, she took me by the hand and glided up the entranceway stairs, pulling me gently alongside her. The stairs opened their way into my living room, where she lay me softly on the floor.

"Sweet one," she began, "close your eyes.

"Now, onward to your experience of breath," Joy continued, her words a blend of comfort and confidence. "Remember always your breath. She is for all time your beautiful doorway, to the land of inner peace that lives within you, just beyond the thin surface of fear you at times hide behind.

"Feel the breath. Feel your lungs fill to greet the incoming air, and then release to make room for the next most wondrous coming. Feel the filling up...and letting go. The coming in...and the release. The taking in of the new...and the release of the old.

"Your breath," she continued, her words a mesmerizing spell, "your most wondrous breath. Feel the rush of air as you take her in, as she arrives first in through your nostrils, as she flows with grace down your windpipe. Then feel her release as you liberate her from the lungs, how she runs to freedom back up through the canal whence she came, to her effortless release through your nostrils.

"At last, feel the rising and falling of your stomach. How she celebrates the coming of new air with her growth, how she falls back with its release.

"Together," Joy continued, putting the pieces of her story together, "feel its unity and its oneness, as the air enters in, gliding her way down through the windpipe...the lungs fill in welcome...the stomach rises in greeting...and then the release...the lungs let go...the stomach relaxes...the air dances her way out through internal tunnels.

"Now, in this very moment," Joy spoke, her words an irresistible combination of calm and clarity, "see deep within you a place of unreasonable compassion and unconditional embrace, and feel yourself drift downward, softly and gently, toward this internal space of splendor.

"Deeper...and deeper still," Joy continued, guiding me on my journey. "In this moment, as always, there is...nowhere to go...and there is...nothing to do. There never has been. Never shall there be." With those words, I felt the last drops of tension in my body give way, and I relaxed completely into the mystery of Joy's words.

"Deeper, now, sweet one...and deeper still...toward the wisdom of your compassion that resides within you. Slowly and gently downward...a return home to the wonder within."

I followed Joy's words to a place deep inside, and I felt an embrace there like never before. There, I was loved in ways beyond the limits of understanding.

As I drifted in this mystical space, I felt a warm glow beside me, and I knew beyond doubt that Joy was by my side. As I looked upward, I saw a star-filled night overflowing with radiance. This was the Night of Infinite Possibility, and here, with Joy, I stood ready for my final adventure.

Chapter 30

Forgetting

As I looked out into the Night of Infinite Possibility, two stars called to me, beckoning me to venture their way. I turned to Joy, unsure of what to do.

"Tonight," she replied softly, "there are two journeys for you to take. Follow your heart and you shall know which is first."

I drifted upward into the night sky, Joy by my side. I trusted that one star would tell me her way was my first choice. My mind argued that there must be a better way to decide than this, but in this land of spirit, my soul knew there was nothing to do but to trust and allow. As the voice of my soul quieted the racket of my mind, as Joy and I floated higher into the night sky, one star grew brighter while the other dimmed, and I knew this was my sign.

I floated toward the starlight expanding with our approach. She welcomed us with the warmth of her light, and, as we drifted nearer, her light quickly filled the sky. Soon, we were embraced by the softness of her welcome. As we drifted within the glow of her space, she transformed herself into a long, radiant tunnel, and she invited us on a graceful journey through her.

Our journey was a long one, as she took us through the pathways of time. I could see the years drifting by, far into the unknowns of the future. When her tunnel gave way to its end, and she prepared to release us, I knew we had journeyed thirty years into what might be.

We emerged from her embrace, Joy and I, and found ourselves floating gently in the quiet of night sky.

"Where are we, Joy?" I asked, wanting to find my way.

"Sweet one," she said, "we are here in your future, here to visit you."

With that, she pulled gently on my hand and guided me downward to a home just beneath us. We floated toward it and through an open bathroom window. When we landed softly on the tiled floor beneath us, I saw him for the first time.

He stood before me, his strong features, big piercing eyes, the large sculpted nose, long thick eyebrows, all unmistakable signposts. This was *me* I was looking at, thirty years into the future. His hairline had continued on a path started some thirty years ago, receding rapidly along the top of his head until now hardly a trace of the thick black hair remained.

The more I looked, the more discomfort I felt. There was something terribly wrong here.

His forehead was lined with wrinkles, as was much of his face. His eyes were turned downward, as if weighted down by some burden carried through all his years. His face had a sadness in it, revealing a somberness that lived within. Even the shape his body and his very posture seemed distorted. He slouched, afraid to stand tall and proud. His stomach carried extra weight, which he tried to hide under a layer of oversized shirts, one of the many of side effects of a body neglected through the passing years.

The future me looked at himself in a full-body mirror, brushing back the little hair that remained with him all these years. He stepped back, seeking a full-body view. As he caught sight of himself in the mirror, his face was colored with disappointment. He muttered an incriminating, "How could I have let this happen?"

The sounds of a car arriving in his driveway diverted his attention from his misery, if only momentarily. He hurried out of the bathroom to reply to the calling of the sounds.

"Joy, what's going on here?" I asked. "Why do I look so sad? My whole face and body look distorted by an unhappiness that I'm carrying. Did someone die and I never get over it?"

"In a manner of speaking," Joy replied in calming words, seeing a sense of panic growing within me, "someone has died. But that someone was you."

"What?"

"Sweet one, this is the future where you never got around to changing the belief: 'There must be something wrong with me.' This is the future where you spent the next thirty years of your life forgetting the wonder of who you are, the perfection and the marvel of you, the Divinity that is your birthright.

"You started with the best of intentions when I left you thirty years ago to the day. 'I'll remember Joy's words,' you declared to yourself every night. 'I'll remember to live with intention. I'll remember the Difference of Persistence, the Attitude of Gratitude. I'll live a life well beyond the illusions of judgment,' you announced."

"What happened?" I asked.

"You forgot. You claimed, 'Life got in my way.' You allowed yourself to get so busy first with getting work done, then with pleasing your current partner, and finally with keeping your kids happy, you stopped taking the time out to take care of yourself. You forgot that the greatest gift you could give your work, the greatest gift you could give your wife, the greatest gift you could give your kids, was a joyful, loving you. What more could anyone ever ask than that? Yet you fell back into the illusions of the world. You decided that all things other than joy were your number one priority. And so you hurried through your life, trying to get it *all* done. In hurrying, you returned to old patterns, and you forgot."

"But Joy, how could I ever forget you?"

"You never did, dear one. But as time drifted forward, I felt more like a distant memory of a time long ago. Sometimes at night, when you felt your day had worked against you, you sat up late into the night, calling my name, beckoning me to return to you. When I did not, you decided that I had abandoned you. And so, in your heart, you abandoned me, too."

"But, Joy, why didn't you come when I called you in those nights? Why weren't you there for me?"

"Dearest, know now and forever more the truth of these words. I am always there for you. I shall never, ever abandon you. It is just that I shall not always manifest myself in the way you would choose. Always shall I live within you. All you need ever do is look within, and the wisdom that you seek from me shall be found there."

"But, Joy," I argued, "even without you, creating Joy isn't so hard. Not with the invention of Intention. All I have to do is turn everyday events into spiritual experiences. Like every time the phone rings, I use the first two rings as a reminder of my intention to make joy my number one priority. How could I forget *that?*"

"In the hurry through life, all things are forgotten. You decide that the work is the most important thing; that the money is the most important thing; that taking care of someone else before you take care of yourself is most important. In all those moments, you forget to nurture your joy, and the telephone ring becomes an everyday experience once again."

"Joy," I declared, as if a vow to myself and all the world, "I shall never forget what you've taught me."

Joy smiled softly in reply, then signaled for me to follow her.

"Come," she said, "there is more for you to see here." I was more than ready to leave this time and place, but I trusted Joy implicitly. If she said there was more to see, then I would see it.

We glided out of the bathroom, down a long hallway, and then down a flight of stairs to the front entrance. We arrived just in time to see the future me, the me who had abandoned nurturing a belief in my wonder, opening the door.

There she was again, the very same woman I had married in my vision of a wedding.

"Joy," I began, "am I still married to her?"

She nodded in reply, indicating that indeed I was.

My greeting of my wife revealed what a thousand words could not. The greeting was tentative, a small hug, a brief embrace. There was a love between them, but it seemed measured. It was as if love was available only in limited supplies, and I was being careful how much I dished out, not wanting to overdraw on my love account.

As my wife walked by the future me, a child followed her through the entrance door.

He was eight or nine years old. He wore a big smile and grinned broadly at the sight of the future me, his father. I watched as father picked up his son and held him. The boy loved his father freely, but the father seemed willing to dish out love in only limited supplies. Despite the warmth of the father's embrace, I could see him hold back from the fullness of his hug. He was embarrassed to love someone too much.

"Joy, what's happening?" I asked. "Why am I so tentative in my love for these people?"

"Sweet one, the degree to which you are willing to give love to yourself is the degree to which you can give to another. You have, in this future, held back the floodgates of love you have for yourself, deciding you are not worthy of that degree of love. As you do with yourself, so too do you do with those around you.

"You are loving them to the best of your ability, just as you are loving yourself to the best of your ability. But your ability to love is limited by what you believe."

"This is terrible," I thought to myself.

"No, sweet one," Joy replied, answering my thoughts, "it is neither good nor bad. It is just one way. The question for you is not, 'How could I have let this happen?' Beyond the limits of judgment, the question becomes, 'What are you to create from this?'"

I knew I never wanted this future to come into being. I knew this was far from all I ever wanted for myself.

"In life," I declared, "there are anchoring moments. Things we remember all our lives that shape who we become. I declare that this my anchoring moment. I will remember here and now.

"In remembering, I'm going to remind myself that in every moment I have a choice to make: 'Do I want Joy in this moment?' Every time my answer is no, the simple consequence is that I move myself closer to this reality.

"Joy," I announced, my energy renewed by my promise, "if I am seeing this future, then I also want to see..." I was going to tell her how much I wanted to see the future in which I *did* change my belief, where I nurtured in my life the perception that I was wondrous just as I was, where I liberated myself to be the Divinity that was my birthright. But it was then I remembered there were two journeys for me to take on this night, two stars who had called. I smiled at Joy, ready for my second journey.

She took my hand in reply, and together we floated out of one possible future, and into the night sky, a Night of Infinite Possibilities.

Chapter 31

The Alternative

As we floated upward, I felt starlight calling me once again. There in the night sky was a twinkling gem calling my name. We drifted heavenward toward her beckoning, Joy's hand in mine. We moved toward the summoning in the sky.

Starlight grew in greeting as we approached, and we were warmed by her welcome. As we entered into her embrace, she led us down the doorways of possibility. Somehow, without words, my soul knew that we were still thirty years into my future, traveling now to an altogether different reality. As we emerged from the light, we once again found ourselves floating in a delightful night sky.

A warm summer breeze filled the night air, and Joy and I floated effortlessly, carried gently by her currents. Soon, as we passed over a large house aglow in a field of sunflowers, Joy tugged my hand, and we began to float downward toward her.

We entered once again through an open bathroom window. It was there I saw him for the first time.

He stood with confidence in front of a full-body bathroom mirror. His features were once again unmistakably my own: the dark penetrating eyes, the thick brows defining them, the slender strong nose that cascaded down a well-defined face. There he stood, a vision of me altered by a very different thirty years. His hairline had surrendered its receding ways, and I could see strong black hair still alive on the top of his head.

Everything seemed very right in this space and time. As I studied his face, it seemed almost untouched by the passage of years. A few wrinkles, the product of years of laughter rather than years of worry, spotted his otherwise smooth skin. His eyes were aglow with confidence, and they looked like living doorways to the depth of his soul. As his face relaxed, it offered an upward turn, his lips turned lightly skyward, a small smile of celebration covering his face. This was, beyond a doubt, a face that had been shaped by years of jubilee.

He stood before the full-body mirror, content with the way he looked. He brushed his hair back with his hand, as if wanting to create an even grander version of himself. He stood tall and proud, his back raised and his shoulders relaxed, the image of a man at home in his body. His chest, stomach, and legs were all gently shaped, framing the outline of a man who took care of the body he called home.

The sounds of a car arriving in his driveway called for his attention, and he headed out of the bathroom. Confident, self-assured strides formed his every step.

Joy and I followed him through a hallway that lead to his front door. We watched, when he opened it, as his face turned the color of delight.

There she was again, a vision of the woman I had seen myself marry.

He greeted her with the warmest embrace I had ever seen. He hugged her fully and deeply, loving her with the fullness of his soul. While she was still in his embrace, he picked her up and spun her joyfully as she screamed with excitement. It was the most wondrous of moments. Joy uninterrupted.

He put her down gently, freeing her from the passion of his hug. They laughed together, both aglow in their togetherness.

Behind her came a child, perhaps twelve years old. His eyes lit up with the colors of pleasure, and as freely as he had loved his wife just moments ago, so too did he embrace his daughter. With the fullness of his hug, he picked her up and spun her around the room.

"Dad," she protested weakly, laughing as she spoke, "you know I'm too old for this."

He ignored her words, loving her all the more with his embrace in the face of them. He reminded me of Joy, his love so abundant and generous. It was as if he knew the very secret of love: The more you give it away, the more you receive in kind. This was a man who loved freely, and who was freely loved.

"Joy," I said, the sense of awe in all I saw awake in my voice, "this could be me?"

"Of course, dear one," Joy replied, her delight in showing me this world of possibility apparent in her tones. "This is the life lived when you nurture the wonder of all that you are. This is the life where you have lived your Inventions of Intention, your Insistence on Persistence, the Attitude of Gratitude, and practiced experiencing beyond the limits of judgment. Through all this practice, you have nurtured the knowing of your soul. And your soul, in response, has nurtured you.

"You have come to believe, still not in all the moments, but in so many that you can not count anymore, that you are indeed Divine. Alive in you is your magnificence and your perfection.

"You live now from the wisdom within. Living in this way, you trust yourself to love fully both yourself and all those around you. Life, for you, has been transformed. She is becoming the Dream of Delight she was always meant to be."

"Joy," I announced, "I want to remember my time here always, and in all ways. I can become this! Every time a moment in life invites me, 'Would you like to be joyful now?', I'll remember the miraculous consequence of saying yes. With every yes, I'll move one step closer to this abundant life."

"Of course, dear one. How else can it be? Remember your

vision of this time, always. For she shall help guide you through your lifetime."

With those words, Joy took me by the hand, and we headed out through an open window, and upward into a night sky. The stars were aglow above, in a Night of Infinite Possibility.

We floated up into the heavens, an ocean of painted dots on a canvas of black. Each star smiled at us that night, as if to thank us for our time in her sky. And there I saw her, one shining more brightly than all those by her side, calling to us with her twinkling.

We drifted gently toward her, excited by the promise of a warm embrace. As we drew nearer, she surrounded us with her welcome. Soon, we were embraced by her light. As we drifted though her passages, I could feel our movement back through the doorways of time, a gentle return to the time I called home. Soon, her long, soothing passageways neared their end, and as we emerged from the light, I felt myself alive to the sensations of my body. I began to move my body slowly, telling it gently of the return of mind and soul.

It was then I felt Joy's words within me.

"Remember, dearest one," the words began, spoken with the warmth and softness that characterized Joy's presence in all our time together. "You are a child of the Universe, no less than the trees and the stars—you have a right to be here. You, like the trees, have a right to stand tall and proud. You, like the stars, have a right to let the light of your wonder shine through you. Within you lies the ability to create all this. Within you lives the courage to believe in yourself. Nurture the wonder of who you are and all that you ever imagined—no, more than you could ever imagine—shall be yours to behold and delight.

"I shall never leave you, not now, not ever. Always shall I live within you, in the perfection that you really are."

ABOUT THE AUTHOR

Dr. Carl R. Nassar lives in Fort Collins, Colorado, with his wife Gretchen and their two cats, Sage and Rita.

Carl is founder and director of The Miracle Center, where he teaches people how to live the empowering ideas shared throughout *The Spirit of Joy.*

Carl's work at The Miracle Center includes supporting individuals, couples, and families as a counselor and coach, as well as leading uplifting workshops and seminars.

In all that he does, Carl helps people remember that the greatest miracle of all lives within: the ability to love and be happy.

To contact Carl, please write or call

Carl R. Nassar
The Miracle Center
141 S. College Ave. Suite 213
Fort Collins, CO 80524
(877) WAY-2JOY
joy@miraclecenter.com

WORDS OF GRATITUDE FOR THE SUPPORT OF

Shanti Bennett, Cover Artist
Shanti brought The Spirit of Joy alive in imagery through her beautiful 3-foot by 4-foot oil painting which graces the front cover (in smaller size).

To order your own limited edition reprint of The Spirit of Joy, please contact Shanti at (970)-229-9269 or reach her by e-mail through The Miracle Center at joy@miraclecenter.com.

Also, feel free to contact Shanti to commission her for your own projects or to see a listing of her other works.

Sue Collier, Cover Design and Layout, Book Design
Sue put words and imagery together to create the sweet book that appears before you now. Her patience and commitment to excellence are greatly appreciated. To talk with Sue regarding your project, please call (970) 482-0318 or e-mail Sue@LeadDogCommunications.com.

The Readers and Reviewers of this Book
Thanks to those of you who boldly held the first draft in your hands, then thoughtfully read and responded: Jenny Briggs, Sarita Crawford, Debbie Killeen, Claudia Merwin, Brenda Rader Mross, Tara Wells, Mark Cochran, Leslie Kaner, Debbie Slevin, Judy Summers, Lois Offenberg, Gretchen Brooks Nassar, Shanti Bennett, Christine Nassar, Annie Sepulveda, Melisa Guire, and Marion Agnew.

BRINGING THE IDEAS IN THE BOOK TO LIFE

THE MIRACLE CENTER
141 S. College Ave.
Fort Collins, CO 80524 USA
Phone: (877) WAY-2JOY
Phone: (970) 498-0709
www.MiracleCenter.com

Hi, I'm Dr. Carl R. Nassar, the author of this book and the director of The Miracle Center. Soon after my experiences with Joy, I decided that the wonder she blessed me with was not meant for me alone, but was meant to be shared with the world around me.

With that in mind, I founded The Miracle Center, located in Fort Collins, Colorado. There, I work with people one-on-one and teach workshops and seminars to share the empowering ideas given to me.

Our workshops include

Overjoyed! Creating Joy in Everyday Life

Living From the Heart   The Gifts of Compassion

Thriving on Life   Awakening to the Empowered You

The Joys of Togetherness   A Workshop for Couples

For a free quarterly newsletter, and a free catalogue, please call or write The Miracle Center.

THIS BOOK IS YOURS FREE

The Miracle Center would like to
encourage and support you in tapping
into the well-spring of Joy that lives within.

Sign up for a workshop, seminar, or individual session (by
phone or in person) with The Miracle Center and you'll be
reimbursed the full cost of this book.

Call or write us today for a free catalogue.

(877) WAY-2JOY

The Miracle Center
141 S. College Ave.
Fort Collins, CO 80524

DON'T JUST READ THIS BOOK, LIVE IT!

Be sure to order the transformational CD

The Spirit of Joy

Meditations to Awaken the Soul

This CD welcomes you to your own personal
journeys with Joy.

It begins with a brief introduction by the author as well as
Joy herself.

Joy then takes you on three, 20 minute guided journeys.

Each journey is an invitation to personal transformation,
to making the changes you read in this book come
alive in your life.

Don't just read this book, LIVE IT!

Call (877) WAY-2JOY or go online to
www.MiracleCenter.com and order your CD today.

ALSO FROM MIRACLE BOOKS

By Carl R. Nassar

Five Habits for Happiness
Create Joy in Your Everyday Life
audio cassette or CD

Discover five surprisingly simple yet incredibly effective habits that empower you to experience joy regardless of external circumstance. Learn how to integrate these five tools into your life and create a happiness that lasts a lifetime. You'll learn:

Joy Unlimited: tap into your ability to choose your response to the events of your life, and turn tears into triumph;

Adversity Transformed: flip from adversity to opportunity, and from hardship to inspiration;

A Life Fully Lived: bring a commitment to excellence to everything you do;

From Ordinary to Extraordinary: discover and delight in the fullness of everyday life.

Don't just read this book, LIVE IT!

Call (877) WAY-2JOY or go online to www.MiracleCenter.com and order your copy today.

Cassette $9.95 CD $12.95